SEMEIA 20

Pronouncement Stories

Editor of this Issue:
Robert C. Tannehill

82021014

Distributed by
SCHOLARS PRESS
101 Salem Street
P.O. Box 2268
Chico, CA 95927

Printed in the United States of America

1 2 3 4 5

Edwards Brothers, Inc.
Ann Arbor, MI 48104

CONTENTS

CONTRIBUTORS TO THIS ISSUE

John E. Alsup
   Austin Presbyterian Theological Seminary
   100 East 27th Street
   Austin, Texas 78705

Leonard Greenspoon
   Department of History
   Clemson University
   Clemson, South Carolina 29631

Pheme Perkins
   Department of Theology
   Boston College
   Chestnut Hill, Massachusetts 02167

Gary G. Porton
   Program for Religious Studies
   4016A Foreign Languages Building
   University of Illinois
   Urbana, Illinois 6180

Paula Nassen Poulos
   2232 Lofty Heights Place
   Reston, Virginia 22091

Vernon K. Robbins
   Program for Religious Studies
   4016 Foreign Languages Building
   University of Illinois
   Urbana, Illinois 61801

William D. Stroker
   Department of Religion
   Drew University
   Madison, New Jersey 07940

Robert C. Tannehill
   Methodist Theological School in Ohio
   Delaware, Ohio 43015

James C. VanderKam
   Department of Philosophy and Religion
   North Carolina State University
   Raleigh, North Carolina 27650

INTRODUCTION: THE PRONOUNCEMENT STORY AND ITS TYPES

Robert C. Tannehill
Methodist Theological School in Ohio

ABSTRACT

After defining pronouncement story, this essay discusses how such stories are rhetorically shaped to influence their readers and how a useful typology of pronouncement stories can be constructed. Six types of pronouncement stories are defined and illustrated so that readers will understand the typology employed in the following studies of various ancient literature.

1.   The name "pronouncement story," coined by Vincent Taylor (29–30, 63–87), will be used to designate the literary genre discussed in this volume. This name is immediately descriptive, indicating the two characteristic parts of the genre, a *pronouncement* which is the climactic element in a brief *story*. As used here, pronouncement story will correspond rather closely with Rudolf Bultmann's "apophthegms" (Bultmann: 8–73. E.T. 11–69) and less closely with Martin Dibelius' "paradigms" (Dibelius: 24–25, 34–66. E.T. 26, 37–69). It also overlaps with the *chreia* discussed by some ancient scholars (see Lausberg: 536–540).

1.1   A pronouncement story is a brief narrative in which the climactic (and often final) element is a pronouncement which is presented as a particular person's response to something said or observed on a particular occasion of the past. There are two main parts of a pronouncement story: the pronouncement and its setting, i.e., the response and the situation provoking that response. The movement from the one to the other is the main development in these brief stories.

1.11   Brevity is a relative matter, of course. In some cases a pronouncement story is a single sentence, with the occasion indicated in a subordinate clause and the response in the main clause. However, a pronouncement story can be longer without losing its basic characteristics. Descriptive detail can be added, and several exchanges of dialogue can take place. It remains a pronouncement story so long as the description and dialogue lead on to a climactic utterance which summarizes the responder's response to the situation. This utterance must be the dominant element in the story as a whole. Preceding material will lead up to it, and it will bring the story to a close or, at most, be followed by a brief indication of the effect of the utterance. There are also some stories in which the utterance is accompanied by action, word and action together constituting the response (see below 1.12). A longer, more complex story may be a sign that other interests are competing with the final utterance. A number of exchanges between characters in the story may indicate that a number of points are being made about a topic, decreasing the dominance of the final utterance and suggesting that we have a short dialogue rather than a pronouncement story. On the other hand, these exchanges may simply prepare for the climactic utterance. In the synoptic Gospels a pronouncement story up to ten verses in length is not unusual, and there are a few that are longer. There are pronouncement stories of comparable length in non-Christian authors /1/. The test of dominance is important in deciding whether a story is a pronouncement story. Is there an utterance at or near the end of the story which dominates the story as a whole because the rest of the story leads up to it and contributes to the impression which it makes? If so, we probably have a pronouncement story.

1.12   The pronouncement itself is usually short, often a single sentence, and is sometimes strikingly succinct in expression. But a response of three or more sentences is possible, provided that it makes a single major point related to the provoking occasion. On the other hand, a general discourse in a lengthy paragraph or a series of separate sayings roughly equal in importance suggests that we have moved outside the pronouncement story genre. There are some pronouncement stories in which the response consists of a pronouncement accompanied by an action. The two together constitute the response and indicate the attitude of the responder. Ancient scholars recognized this possibility in discussing the types of *chreia* (see Lausberg: 539). They also noted that an expressive action might take the place of an utterance (Lausberg: 538–539). Such cases are rare, however, and they have not caused me to abandon the convenient designation pronouncement story. In such stories the expressive action is given the role usually reserved for the dominant utterance: it is the climactic disclosure of a significant response for which the rest of the story provides the provoking occasion. As Lausberg says, "The action has semantic purpose like a pronouncement" (538).

1.13   A pronouncement story is meaningful in itself and can stand alone. We find collections of them which make no attempt to provide a narrative bridge from one story to the next /2/. A pronouncement story may also be embedded in an essay or speech, or form an episode in a larger narrative. In the latter case, the pronouncement story remains meaningful in itself, even though it may gain added meaning through its function in the larger plot of the narrative. Its relative independence is usually indicated by a shift in some characters and/or a shift in time or place before and after the pronouncement story. This marks the scene as an occasion separate from other occasions.

1.2   The pronouncement story is stylized and should not be confused with a complete and neutral report of an actual conversation. Some conversations may be as brief as the average pronouncement story and end with a memorable statement, but most conversations are longer, and even if a striking statement is occasionally made, it seldom ends the matter. The pronouncement story is highly selective in what it presents. In most cases we are told only those details of the situation which help to make the response understandable and impressive. This is an indication that the pronouncement story is rhetorically shaped. The story teller has shaped the story to make an impression on the hearer or reader. The parties in the story are not given an equal hearing. The pronouncement of the one person is placed in climactic position in the story so that it will make the dominant impression. The rest of the story points forward to this pronouncement, which is being recommended by the story teller for admiration and emulation. The pronouncement itself is often expressed in forceful and memorable language. Since it is usually the end of the story, it makes the final impression on the reader or hearer, without the distraction of statements which qualify or contradict.

1.21   To recognize that a pronouncement story is a form of influence exercised by the story teller upon an audience is, in a sense, to "unmask" the story teller. It is comparable to moving from a naive reaction to a play to the realization that persons have staged these events with an audience in mind, whether the drama is fiction or represents the dramatic shaping of historical events. Such unmasking should not lead us to reject all such forms of influence as illegitimate. Influence is a pervasive and necessary aspect of human communication. When we communicate with other persons, we not only convey ideas but also exercise influence on those persons. Such influence has its dangers: it may manipulate others for the benefit of the manipulator. But it may also be the way in which one person helps another to grow, gaining new insight into the possibilities of humanness. While the pronouncement story may contain brief arguments, most of these stories are so brief and so shaped to increase the rhetorical impact of the dominant utterance that there is little room for rational argument. Still, the forceful words, made more forceful by their setting, can provoke a new way of seeing things. They can stimulate imaginative thought along lines previously neglected or rejected. Although the appeal may be as much to the imagination and the will as to the reason, reason has a rightful role in assessing a pronouncement and unfolding its implications. But reason itself is impoverished if it is not stimulated by words which work in the imagination. Without such stimulus the past will dictate to the present what it must think. Thus the imaginative impact of these little dramatic scenes, including the rhetorical force of the climactic utterance, can contribute to the value and importance of pronouncement stories /3/.

1.22   The direction of the influence being exercised through the story is clarified if we consider the relation between the setting and the dominant pronouncement, or between the stimulus (the situation which provokes the pronouncement) and the response. The climactic response, by its position in the story and often by its forceful expression, is being recommended to the reader (unless we have a pronouncement story parody). Commonly it expresses an attitude which the story teller regards as admirable and exemplary, though occasionally the pronouncement is valued simply because it is funny. In many cases this attitude contrasts with another attitude, sometimes expressed or represented by another character in the story, sometimes indicated in another way or presupposed from the social setting of the story. The various forms of contrast enable the story to express an attitudinal shift. The reader or hearer is being invited to follow this shift, rejecting one attitude and embracing another. It is useful to speak of attitudes here in order to indicate that more than the intellect is involved. A basic attitude includes value commitments, emotional attachments, the orientation of the will, and evaluative thought. Such attitudes shape personal life at a deep level, and a shift in basic attitudes can deeply affect the self. The interpreter of pronouncement stories should be alert to the movement from one attitude to another which many of these stories invite. This will help the interpreter to understand the purpose of the rhetorical shaping of the story and the pronouncement. It will also help us to understand more clearly how pronouncement stories reflect the value conflicts of the ancient world (see further Tannehill, 1980).

1.3   The discussion of synoptic pronouncement stories has been and continues to be heavily influenced by the work of Rudolf Bultmann and Martin Dibelius. It is unfortunate that the study of the pronouncement story and its types has made little progress since their important work. The discussions which follow will show that a new understanding of the types of pronouncement story is both possible and useful. Dibelius did not attempt to classify paradigms into types. Bultmann did divide his apophthegms into three classes: the controversy dialogues, the scholastic dialogues, and the biographical apophthegms. The last of these appears to be a miscellaneous grouping without clear formal definition, and Bultmann overlooked significant similarities and differences among texts in classifying them as he did. Renewed consideration of the types of pronouncement story will allow us to clarify further the functions for which the various types are fitted. Furthermore, Bultmann was primarily interested in the history of the pre-Gospel tradition. While that is a legitimate interest, it is also important to consider pronouncement stories as we find them in ancient texts, seeking to understand them as acts of communication between writers and readers. This is the controlling interest here. It should also be apparent that the following studies represent a much broader investigation of pronouncement stories in ancient literature than Bultmann and Dibelius were able to present in their discussion of parallels to synoptic stories. This broad investigation is the result of cooperative research by members of the Pronouncement Story Work Group, sponsored by the Society of Biblical Literature /4/.

1.31   The typology employed in most of the following essays emerges from the definition of pronouncement story given above (see 1.1). There are two necessary parts to a pronouncement story, the response and the situation which provokes that response. A system of types emerges when we consider the various ways in which the provoking occasion and the response are related to each other in groups of pronouncement stories. These two main parts of a pronouncement story are correlative, i.e., the function of the one part must correlate with the function of the other or the story will be malformed and confusing. Each part must be understood in relation to the other and that relationship can be defined. When large groups of pronouncement stories are examined with this in mind, a useful system of types can be developed. The two main parts of a pronouncement story can be discerned even in stories that are relatively long for the genre. The response begins when the responder (the one who will utter the climactic pronouncement which settles the matter as far as the story is concerned) takes charge of the situation and begins to move toward the climactic pronouncement, even if there are some preliminary steps before the climax.

1.32   The stimulating occasion may include dialogue addressed to the responder or it may not. The responder may simply respond to something observed. This in itself does not determine the function of the first part of the story. Furthermore, the presence of a question addressed to the responder does not tell us how the question functions in a particular story. The responder may accept it as a legitimate request for instruction and respond accordingly, but the question may also express an objection, announce a quest, or express an assumption which the responder will correct.

1.33   Construction of a typology based on the relation of the stimulating occasion and the response has the advantage of focusing on a feature which is essential to the pronouncement story as such. It directs our attention to the pronouncement story as a whole, rather than defining types on the basis of a part considered in isolation. It focuses on the main development in the story, the movement which makes the story a story. The stimulating occasion creates suspense and expectation in the reader, who will want to know what is going to happen as a result. The response discloses the result. Each of the types listed below corresponds to a particular kind of movement from stimulus to response. Furthermore, this way of defining the types can provide clues to the rhetorical function of the story, the way in which the story teller is seeking to influence the reader. The interaction between stimulus and response may reflect or anticipate types of interaction between the reader and the story. Recognizing this will help us to understand the purpose of the shaping of both story and pronouncement. This approach can also contribute to our knowledge of the ancient world. The tension within a story may reflect the interaction of a person or group with the surrounding world, at least as pictured by the group that regards the dominant utterance as valuable and, perhaps, normative. The stories not only disclose the ideals that are being promoted by certain persons and groups but may also mirror the perceived conflict between these ideals and other attitudes in the ancient world. Something of the value conflicts of the time shine through. Definition of the movement from stimulating occasion to response in the story can aid us in understanding how the stories reflect these conflicts. Finally, this typology can increase the value of comparative study of pronouncement stories in various literatures of the ancient world. It allows us to compare the relative frequency of use of the different types in various documents, note unusual variations within the types, and recognize how the interaction basic to each type can be employed to express the special concerns and values of particular religious, philosophical, and cultural perspectives as they interact with the surrounding world.

2.   The following types of pronouncement stories appear when we study the relation between the stimulating occasion and the response in each story: 1) correction stories (or simply "corrections"), 2) commendation stories ("commendations"), 3) objection stories ("objections"), 4) quest stories ("quests"), 5) inquiry stories ("inquiries"), 6) description stories ("descriptions"). I cannot claim that these types encompass all of the pronouncement stories in the literature of the ancient Mediterranean world. However, these types, or combinations of them (see 2.7 below on "hybrids"), fit a large number of these pronouncement stories. The names of the types appear to relate to one part of the pronouncement story, either the stimulus or the response. However, they actually describe the pronouncement story as a whole, since the parts are correlative. In corrections and commendations it is the response which corrects or commends, but this implies a stimulus in which someone has taken a position by word or action which can be corrected or commended. Objections, quests, and inquiries have names that refer most clearly to the stimulus part of the story, but in each case there must be a response appropriate to the type. Indeed, only the response can make clear how the initial situation is relevant and functional in the story.

I will now describe the types of pronouncement story more carefully and give an example of each type.

2.1   *Correction stories.* In a correction story the responder corrects someone whose actions or words are presented in the stimulus part of the story. By action, by outright statement, or by implication from something said, someone has taken a position as to what is right or expedient, and the responder corrects that position. Thus two attitudes are contrasted in correction stories. Because of the dominant and final position of the response, as well as its rhetorical force in many cases, the attitude expressed there will make the chief impression on the reader. It is being recommended in contrast to the attitude being corrected. The responder may respond to something observed without being addressed by the one who is corrected, or the response may be part of a dialogue in which the responder replies to a statement, request, or question from the one corrected. In the case of requests and questions, the responder does not grant the request or answer the question but corrects an assumption on which the request or question was based. The correction causes tension between the corrector and the one being corrected. This tension does not become clear in the story until the response is made. Thus the development is different from that in objection stories, which may also involve a corrective response. In objection stories an objection is raised against the responder and this provokes the response. Thus tension appears already in the stimulus part, and the responder has a personal interest in the reply, having to defend previous words or actions. In a correction story, however, the position adopted in the stimulus is not an objection against the responder. The position taken may seem innocent, perhaps even commendable. It may represent common practice and ordinary values. The reader may initially agree with or tolerate such a practice and such values. But the story opens up distance between such views and the position of the responder. This also opens up a choice for the reader, which can lead to a shift of attitudes and priorities.

Correction stories are the most common type of pronouncement story in Lucian's *Demonax*, Philostratus' *The Life of Apollonius of Tyana*, Diogenes Laertius' *Lives and Opinions of Eminent Philosophers*, and (pseudo?)-Plutarch's *Sayings of Kings and Commanders*. Corrections represent a large share of the pronouncement stories found in non-Christian Greek literature of the Roman period. An example from Lucian, *Demonax* 27 (trans. A. M. Harmon):

> When one of his friends said: "Demonax, let's go to the Aesculapium and pray for my son," he replied: "You must think Aesculapius very deaf, that he can't hear our prayers from where we are!"

2.2   *Commendation stories.* Commendations are similar to corrections in that the responder responds to a position taken by another person with an evaluative comment. However, in commendations the responder commends rather than corrects the other person. The response will affirm or praise something said, done, or represented by the other person. This tends to make the person commended into a model to be imitated by others. The responder maintains an important position in the story, being the source of the recommended evaluation, but the one commended also represents positive values in these stories. The shared and stable values of a culture can be reinforced by such stories. However, the response gains in interest when it contains a surprise, i. e., when it is unusual in light of other, common judgments about the matter. In such cases there is an implicit contrast between the commendation and another viewpoint. This contrast may come to expression in the response. It may be strongly expressed, as synoptic commendations often do, through the introduction of a third character into the story who takes a negative view of the one being commended or who acts in a way contrary to the action being commended. In such a case we have a hybrid story, in which two movements typical of pronouncement stories are combined, with the response correcting one person and commending another or replying to an objection from one person and commending another. Thus the commendation story, as well as the correction story, may reveal the competition of values and value judgments at the time and place of its origin. It may disclose a hidden value and importance in a person or attitude which seemed unimportant or contemptible by ordinary standards.

Quest stories may also contain a statement of commendation if the quest is successful. However, in quest stories someone approaches the responder seeking help and the success or failure of this quest is announced at the end of the story. In other words, the suspense created by a quest determines the limits and structure of the story. This is not the case in commendations.

An example of a commendation story from Plutarch, *Sayings of Spartan Women* 241A (trans. F. C. Babbitt, modified):

> Another woman, hearing that her son had fallen on the field of battle, said:
> "Let the poor cowards be mourned, but, with never a tear do I bury
> You, my son, who are mine, yea, and are Sparta's as well."

2.3   *Objection stories.* Objection stories, like correction stories, present a situation of conflict. However, in corrections the conflict is first indicated by the response, while in objections it is created by an objection to the behavior or views of the responder or his followers. The objection story has three parts, though the first two are often combined: 1) the cause of the objection, 2) the objection, which is sometimes expressed by a question asking why something was done or said, and 3) the response to the objection. The cause of the objection may either be narrated prior to the objection or reported as part of the objection. In an objection story the responder is already committed to a position through the words or action causing the objection. The resulting challenge creates tension within the story and puts the responder in a difficult situation. However, an impressive response is all the more impressive because it occurs in a situation of difficulty and risk. The response may correct assumptions on which the objection was based, resembling the response in a correction story in this respect. It may also move the conflict to a basic level, disclosing issues of fundamental priorities and of basic perceptions of truth and value behind the conflict. In my article on "Varieties of Synoptic Pronouncement Stories" later in this volume (see 5.2–5.21) I will refer to a group of testing inquiry stories in the Gospels. These stories are similar to objections in that the suspense of the story focuses on the responder, whose authority is being challenged or tested. The two groups of stories differ, however, for in the testing inquiries the responder is not replying to an objection against a position already taken /5/.

The following example of a brief objection story comes from Diogenes Laertius, *Lives and Opinions of Eminent Philosophers* VI 63:

> To one reproaching him [Diogenes] for entering unclean places he said, "The sun, too, enters the privies but is not defiled."

2.4   *Quest stories.* A pronouncement by the responder is found near the end of a quest story, as in other pronouncement stories, and this pronouncement has a crucial role in the story, for it will determine the success or failure of the quest. However, quests are often more elaborate than other pronouncement stories, and the quester has a more prominent role than most persons encountered by a responder in pronouncement stories. The story concerns a person in quest of something important to human well-being. It begins by introducing the quester and the quest; it ends by indicating the success or failure of the quest. This interest in the outcome of events for the person who encounters the responder is not typical of pronouncement stories in general, but it is a necessary part of a quest story. The story attracts the reader's attention not only to the words of the responder but also to the quester, whose need and desire to fulfill that need provide tension in the story and define its central movement. Because the story focuses attention on the quester's need and awakens interest in the possible fulfillment of that need, it tends to awaken the reader's sympathy. This can heighten the effect of the stories on the reader, making failure seem tragic and success satisfying, even if the questers have some attributes that seem to disqualify them. The responder is the person of authority in the situation, and the quester comes to the responder for help. The responder may pose a difficult condition, or someone may object to the quest. These obstacles are important in the story, for they indicate the issue which is crucial for the outcome of the quest, an issue on which the story teller may wish to change the audience's attitudes. A quest story will not end until we have been informed whether the quester succeeded or failed. A successful quest may end with a statement of commendation by the responder.

Although there is an important group of quest stories in the synoptic Gospels, it has been difficult to find quest stories elsewhere. Therefore, some features of the description above, such as the remarks about the reader's sympathy, may reflect aspects of synoptic stories which do not apply to quest stories elsewhere. Of the few possible quests discovered out-side the Gospels, three are quoted later in this volume, two in the article by Poulos (sect. 2) and one by Alsup (sect. 6). In addition, the following story from Diogenes Laertius, *Lives* VI 96-97 (trans. R. D. Hicks), appears to be a good example of a quest, except that the final sentence merges the successful outcome with following events.

> She [Hipparchia] fell in love with the discourses and the life of Crates, and would not pay attention to any of her suitors, their wealth, their high birth or their beauty. But to her Crates was everything. She used even to threaten her parents she would make away with herself, unless she were given in marriage to him. Crates therefore was implored by her parents to dissuade the girl, and did all he could, and at last, failing to persuade her, got up, took off his clothes before her face and said, "This is the bridegroom, here are his possessions; make your choice accordingly; for you will be no helpmeet of mine, unless you share my pursuits."
>
> The girl chose and, adopting the same dress, went about with her husband . . .

2.5   *Inquiry stories.* An inquiry story moves from a question or request for information to the answer to that question or request. Other types of pronouncement stories may contain questions, but inquiries lack the special features of these other types. The responder does not respond by correcting an assumption on which the question is based, as in a correction story. The question is accepted and an answer is supplied. The question does not express an objection to something already said or done by the responder. It is not the announcement of a quest which is shown to succeed or fail at the end of the story. The dramatic conflict and tension between persons which characterize many of the other stories are largely lacking in the inquiries. What happens to the characters becomes less important, leaving the teaching given by the responder as the remaining matter of importance. The reader's interest focuses almost entirely on the content of the instruction given in the response. Frequently the story setting contributes little to the pronouncement, except that it may introduce the topic being discussed and suggest application of the teaching to a particular group or problem.

The relative lack of dramatic tension in inquiries does not apply to a subtype which I will call testing inquiries. There is an important group of testing inquiries in the synoptic Gospels. I will describe this subtype in the article on "Varieties of Synoptic Pronouncement Stories" (see 5.2).

Inquiries are fairly common in the literature that I have examined, though not as common as corrections. An example from Philostratus, *The Life of Apollonius of Tyana* I xxxvii:

> When the king asked him [Apollonius] how he could rule with stability and security, he said, "Honoring many but trusting few."

2.6   *Description stories.* Description stories begin with a general indi-cation of the situation to which the pronouncement relates. This provides the setting for a comment in which the responder describes the situation, usually in apt and striking language, expressing some remarkable aspect of it. The descriptive comment may be humorous, highlighting something ridiculous or incongruous in the situation. It may also be poignant, highlighting the tragedy of human limitations or the fateful consequences of what has happened. The descriptive response does not answer an inquiry, nor does it positively or negatively evaluate the situation which inspires the comment. Such evaluation would result in a correction or a commendation. The concern for description rather than evaluation is a defining characteristic of the descriptions. While the response may indicate that the situation is incongruous or tragic, it does not imply that it could be otherwise. Rather than saying, "This is not the way it should be; change it," the speaker is saying, "However we may have planned and whatever our desires, this is the way it is." Thus the descriptive response expresses some striking quality of a particular situation. This quality may be unique to the situation, or the situation may manifest a recurrent quality of life.

I offer two examples from (pseudo?)-Plutarch, *Sayings of Kings and Commanders* 185D and 191A (trans. F. C. Babbitt). The first is humorous and applies to a unique situation; the second is poignant and suggests a quality of life in general.

> Of his son, who was pert towards his mother, he [Themistocles] said that the boy wielded more power than anybody else in Greece; for the Athenians ruled the Greeks, he himself ruled the Athenians, the boy's mother ruled himself, and the boy ruled the mother.

> When he [Agesilaus] was about to break camp in haste by night to leave the enemy's country, and saw his favourite youth, owing to illness, being left behind all in tears, he said, "It is hard to be merciful and sensible at the same time."

2.7   As already noted in 2.2 above, several of the types may be combined in a single story to form a hybrid story. In this case the developments from stimulus to response characteristic of several types are found within one story, and the response has more than one function. This may occur when there are only two characters in the story, but it is more likely to occur in stories which present three persons or groups in important roles. The responder may correct one party and commend another, respond to the objection of one party and commend another, respond to an objection and to a quest, etc. In the following example from (pseudo?)-Plutarch, *Sayings of Kings and Commanders* 177A (trans. F. C. Babbitt), Archelaus is both responding to an objection (indicated by the man's astonishment) and commending Euripides.

> When Archelaus, at a convivial gathering, was asked for a golden cup by one of his acquaintances of a type not commendable for character, he bade the servant give it to Euripides; and in answer to the man's look of astonishment, he said, "It is true that you have a right to ask for it, but Euripides has a right to receive it even though he did not ask for it."

2.8   In my article on "Varieties of Synoptic Pronouncement Stories" in this volume, I will apply the typology discussed above to pronouncement stories in the synoptic Gospels and will discuss further the functions of the different types. Most of the other articles in this volume also employ this typology, showing the frequent or infrequent usage of the story types in various ancient literature. In his article on pronouncement stories in four of Plutarch's *Lives*, Robbins proposes some modifications of the typology, and the reader will want to compare Robbins' system with that proposed here. I find his distinction among first, second, and third person corrections and commendations to be a helpful refinement. Calling attention to inverted correction and commendation stories, i.e., stories in which the primary character of the writing as a whole is corrected or commended, rather than correcting or commending, is also helpful. Robbins labels these "rebuffs" and "laudations." Continuing study of pronouncement stories may reveal other types or subtypes, helping us to appreciate the complex possibilities of these seemingly simple stories.

NOTES

/1/   Plutarch provides examples of medium and long pronouncement stories. See the texts quoted in the two essays on Plutarch in this volume.

/2/   See, e. g., (pseudo?)-Plutarch, *Sayings of Kings and Commanders*, and Lucian, *Demonax*.

/3/   On the significance of forceful and imaginative language together with studies of such language in synoptic sayings, see Tannehill, 1975.

/4/   The range of material investigated is not fully represented by the following essays. It includes Philostratus, *Life of Apollonius of Tyana*, *Lives of the Sophists*; Plutarch, *Sayings of Kings and Commanders*, *Sayings of Romans*, *Sayings of Spartans*, *Sayings of Spartan Women*, *Bravery of Women*; and Lucian, *Demonax*. Pronouncement stories in the two works of Philostratus were discussed in a preliminary way by Breech. This was before the methods of the Pronouncement Story Work Group had been clarified. A grant from the National Endowment for the Humanities for a student research assistant helped me to check, organize, and extend the data furnished by other members of the Pronouncement Story Work Group. I am grateful to the National Endowment for the Humanities for this support, and to the student assistant, David D. Wilson, Jr.

/5/   Objection stories correspond to Bultmann's controversy dialogues, but Bultmann obscures the distinction which I wish to make between objections and testing inquiries. While first distinguishing stories which begin with an objection from stories which begin with a question from opponents concerning Jesus' unknown position, Bultmann later includes texts of the latter type in his discussion of controversy dialogues. Compare Bultmann: 9-20, 25-26 with 50-51 (E. T. 12-21, 26-27 with 48-49).

WORKS CONSULTED

Breech, Earl
1977   "Stimulus-Response and Declaratory Pronouncement Stories in Philo-
               stratus." Pp. 257–271 in *Society of Biblical Literature 1977 Seminar
               Papers*. Missoula: Scholars.

Bultmann, Rudolf
1958   *Die Geschichte der synoptischen Tradition*. 4. Aufl. Göttingen:
               Vandenhoeck & Ruprecht. English trans., *The History of the Synoptic
               Tradition*. Rev. ed. New York: Harper & Row, 1968.

Dibelius, Martin
1961   *Die Formgeschichte des Evangeliums*. 4. Aufl. Tübingen: Mohr.
               English trans., *From Tradition to Gospel*. New York: Scribner's.

Lausberg, Heinrich
1973   *Handbuch der literarischen Rhetorik*. 2. Aufl. 2 vols. München: Max
               Hueber.

Tannehill, Robert C.
1975   *The Sword of His Mouth: Forceful and Imaginative Language in
               Synoptic Sayings*. Philadelphia: Fortress, & Missoula: Scholars.

1980   "Attitudinal Shift in Synoptic Pronouncement Stories." Pp. 183–97 in
               Richard A. Spencer (ed.), *Orientation by Disorientation: Studies in
               Literary Criticism and Biblical Literary Criticism in Honor of
               William A. Beardslee*. Pittsburgh: Pickwick.

Taylor, Vincent
1933   *The Formation of the Gospel Tradition*. London: Macmillan.

Sources of Illustrations:

Diogenes Laertius
1950, 1958   *Lives and Opinions of Eminent Philosophers*. 2 vols. LCL.
               Cambridge, Mass.: Harvard University.

Lucian
1953   *Lucian*, vol. 1. LCL. Cambridge, Mass.: Harvard University.

Philostratus
1917, 1921   *The Life of Apollonius of Tyana*. 2 vols. LCL. London: William Hein-
               emann.

Plutarch
1968   *Moralia*, vol. 3. LCL. Cambridge, Mass.: Harvard University.

TYPE, PLACE, AND FUNCTION OF THE PRONOUNCEMENT STORY IN PLUTARCH'S *MORALIA*

John E. Alsup
Austin Presbyterian Theological Seminary

ABSTRACT

A study of Plutarch's *Moralia* provides examples of the six types of pronouncement stories discussed in the "Introduction" to this volume. In this article representative examples are quoted, with brief explanation. Attention is also given to the redactional activity of Plutarch as he makes use of pronouncement stories in the context of his essays and comments upon them. Plutarch's use of pronouncement stories indicates his positive valuation of them as vehicles of educational communication.

0.1   As a member of the Society of Biblical Literature Work Group on Pronouncement Story, I have studied Plutarch's *Moralia* in search of examples of pronouncement stories (hereafter PS) and a satisfactory standard for their classification and analysis. This assignment was shared with Richard A. Spencer. We made use of the volumes of the *Moralia* in the Loeb Classical Library for both text and translation. The division of labor was: vols. 1, 3, 4, 5, and 6: Alsup; vols. 2, 7, 8, 9, and 13: Spencer; vols. 10, 11, 12, 14, and 15: joint responsibility.

0.2   I have made no attempt to present a complete list of the PS in my volumes of the *Moralia*. What follows is a selection of such stories I judge to be representative of the various types found in that work. Reference to PS not quoted and discussed below will be given wherever deemed helpful to the reader.

0.3   Throughout this study I have also become more and more interested in the place of prominence the PS occupied in Plutarch's writings (re: pseudonymous writings, etc., cf. Ziegler). Plutarch was evidently convinced that they were an excellent vehicle for communication and instruction. He wove PS carefully into his own composition and often enlarged upon them with his own commentary; moreover, on occasion he even created PS, I believe, quite freely. It is beyond the scope of this article to discuss the compositional goals of Plutarch himself, but I will note below where his redactional activity has been of some consequence to the form and function of PS.

0.4   While an exact statistical breakdown of each type for the *Moralia* is pending, it is clear that the most numerous types are the objection, correction, commendation, and inquiry, or a hybrid based on some combination. In light of the subject matter of the *Moralia* and its heroes, this concentration of PS type is not surprising. Examples of description and quest are also to be found, however, and will be noted and discussed below.

1.   Objections

1.1   "De Liberis Educandis" I, 4F–5A:

> When a man asked him what fee he should require for teaching his child, Aristippus replied, "A thousand drachmas"; but when the other exclaimed, "Great Heavens! what an excessive demand! I can buy a slave for a thousand," Aristippus retorted, "Then you will have two slaves, your son and the one you buy."

Typical for this type is the objection evoked in response to the main character's solicited reply to initial inquiry. The final pronouncement then provides the justification for that reply or the proof that the (perhaps legitimate) objection is finally overruled by the superior wisdom of the hero/sage. The somewhat cryptic pronouncement in this particular story seems to make the point: learning frees from servitude to ignorance; capable teachers are expensive; fathers are bound morally to provide for their children what the children cannot afford to provide for themselves, namely, the teachers who can lead them to freedom through education. When one adds to this PS the redactional prelude provided by Plutarch himself, this "point" of the story is confirmed:

> Many fathers, however, go so far in their devotion to money as well as in animosity toward their children, that in order to avoid paying a larger fee, they select as teachers for their children men who are not worth any wage at all—looking for ignorance, which is cheap enough. Wherefore Aristippus not inelegantly, in fact very cleverly, rebuked a father who was devoid both of mind and sense. For . . .

To this "point," however, Plutarch adds the disapproving or condemning note that neglect of duty here is often grounded in avarice and animosity. It should also be noted that the disapproving response by Aristippus to the objection is regarded by Plutarch as especially clever or witty, an element which heightens its effectiveness as a vehicle of instruction on suitable behavior for all fathers who would consider the education of their children.

1.2   "De Recta Ratione Audiendi" I, 41D–E:

> He [Dionysius], as it appears, at some performance promised to a harp-player of great repute certain large gifts, but afterwards gave him nothing, on the ground

that he had already discharged his obligation. "For," said he, "all the time that you were giving pleasure to us with your singing, you were enjoying the pleasure of your hopes."

The objection stimulus in this story plays a recessive role in the composition, but a crucial one as the occasion for the pronouncement itself. The reader's expectation supplies the "normal" objection following "afterwards gave him nothing" by converting the next statement into its original form: "Now why don't you discharge your obligation?! You promised large gifts!" The pronouncement justifies—to Plutarch's satisfaction—the countermanding of prior obligation. Whereas the story itself would seem to call for further debate on the means of discerning another's intentions, Plutarch supplies a context for the objection PS fore and aft which precludes that necessity:

... the discussions and exercises of most popular lecturers not only use words to conceal their thoughts, but they so sweeten their voice by certain harmonious modulations and softenings and rhythmic cadences, as to ravish away and transport their hearers. It is an empty pleasure they give, and an even more empty renown they acquire, so that the remark of Dionysius fits their case exactly. For he . . .

—PS—

And this is just the meed that such lectures have for those who deliver them; for the speakers are admired in as far as they are entertaining, and afterwards, no sooner has the pleasure of listening passed away, than their repute deserts them, and so the time of their hearers and the life of the speakers is simply wasted.

1.3   "Regum et Imperatorum Apophthegmata" III, 177A:

When Archelaus, at a convivial gathering, was asked for a golden cup by one of his acquaintances of a type not commendable for character, he bade the servant give it to Euripides; and in answer to the man's look of astonishment, he said, "It is true that you have a right to ask for it, but Euripides has a right to receive it even though he did not ask for it."

Here too the objection is not expressed verbally. It is registered in the look of surprise noted by the narrator. The final pronouncement gives justification for the noncompliance with the initial request. Another element is present in the pronouncement and should be noted: Euripides, who was not involved in the original exchange, has been commended by Archelaus. We may call this an *objection* PS with a *secondary commendation*.

1.4   "Regum et Imperatorum Apophthegmata" III, 177B:

When Timotheus the harp-player had hopes of receiving a goodly sum, but received less, he plainly showed that he felt resentful toward Archelaus; and, once, as he was singing this brief line: "Over the earth-born silver you rave." he directed it towards Archelaus; whereupon Archelaus retorted upon him with this, "That, however, is what you crave."

In contrast to the unexpressed objections above, this PS combines the narrator's interpretation of the objector's hope, the non-verbal objection ("plainly showed . . . "), and the verbal objection placed in direct address. This variation in style is crucial because the formulation of the final justifying pronouncement turns the phrase of the objector and allows Archelaus to emerge as the more clever poet as well.

1.5   "Apophthegmata Laconica" III, 230F:

> When, in Tegea, after he [Pausanius] had been exiled, he commended the Spartans, someone said, "Why did you not stay in Sparta instead of going into exile?" And he said, "Because physicians, too, are wont to spend their time, not among the healthy, but where the sick are."

Here the objection to the commendation of the Spartans is put in direct address and the justifying pronouncement combines several motifs. As in 1.3 there is a commendation of a third party to the story, the Spartans (they are "healthy"). Then there is the disapproving/correcting note regarding the Tegeans (you are deceived if you don't realize you are "sick"). Finally, there is an hortatory note that the Tegeans should take heart because a willing physician is in their midst who will concern himself with their health.

1.6   "Apophthegmata Laconica" III, 234A–B:

> In the case of another boy, when the time had arrived during which it was the custom for the free boys to steal whatever they could, and it was a disgrace not to escape being found out, when the boys with him had stolen a young fox alive, and given it to him to keep, and those who had lost the fox came in search for it, the boy happened to have slipped the fox under his garment. The beast, however, became savage and ate through his side to the vitals; but the boy did not move or cry out, so as to avoid being exposed, and later, when they had departed, the boys saw what had happened, and blamed him, saying that it would have been better to let the fox be seen than to hide it even unto death; but the boy said, "Not so, but better to die without yielding to the pain than through being detected because of weakness of spirit to gain a life to be lived in disgrace."

This rather bizarre PS contains much more narrative detail prior to the objection and final response than is customarily the case. It does not appear that the narrative detail is to be ascribed to the redactional activity of Plutarch. The story is quite homogeneous. The objection is placed in indirect discourse and the justifying pronouncement at the end articulates the Spartan ideal of courage in terms approaching the eloquence of Simonides' epitaph at Thermopylae. This commendatory note of the Spartan ideal—even among the children—is a particularly strong motif here when it comes to the didactic function of the story. As is seen elsewhere in the *Moralia*, Plutarch has the highest regard for Spartan bravery and character.

2.   Corrections

2.1   "De Liberis Educandis" I, 2A:

> Diogenes, observing an emotional and crack-brained youth, said, "Young man, your
> father must have been drunk when he begot you!"

There is a certain deflected quality about this correction PS, for while Diogenes clearly disapproves of the activity of the youth, he does not directly correct his behavior; rather he speaks of the youth's father disapprovingly. The force of the correction, however, is clearly to reprimand the youth about that over which he has some control and to urge him to change his ways (he can hardly change the realities of his conception!). For Plutarch, on the other hand, this PS functions less as correction of the youth than as a warning to future fathers. For him the youth, his problem, and the implicit exhortation to change his ways recede and an introductory observation about life comes to the fore as the unacceptable behavior is itself interpreted as drunkenness:

> For children whose fathers have chanced to beget them in drunkenness are wont to
> be fond of wine, and to be given to excessive drinking. Wherefore . . .

2.2   "Quomodo Adulator ab Amico Internoscatur" I, 70C–D:

> Excellent, too, was the retort of Diogenes on the occasion when he had entered
> Philip's camp and was brought before Philip himself, at the time when Philip was
> on his way to fight the Greeks. Not knowing who Diogenes was, Philip asked him if
> he were a spy. "Yes, indeed, Philip," he replied, "I am here to spy upon your ill-
> advised folly, because of which you, without any compelling reason, are on your
> way to hazard a kingdom and your life on the outcome of a single hour."

At first glance it appears that this is an inquiry or perhaps a hybrid correcting inquiry, but upon closer examination of motif function it would classify as a straightforward correction. The question stimulus (indirect address) for the response of Diogenes is the occasion for a correction and not simply information. The category "spy" as understood by Philip is corrected and given the philosophical connotation of one who inquires into the folly of another person. In reality, "spy upon" moves to the level of "advise against" this undertaking. This hortatory function of the PS, which we have noted on occasion above, is original to the story itself and has not been added as a redactional feature by Plutarch. As in 2.1 the person being corrected is indirectly urged to follow up on the correction with an alteration of behavior.

2.3   "Quomodo Adulator ab Amico Internoscatur" I, 71E:

> Lysander, we are told, said to the man from Megara, who in the council of the
> allies was making bold to speak for Greece, that "his words needed a country to
> back them";

Here the response evoked by the action and words of the "man from Megara" quite directly challenges the assumptions of the speaker and by correcting puts an end to further discussion. Plutarch, however, adds a comment immediately which elevates the pronouncement to the maxim: let frank speech be backed by character!

so it may well be that every man's frank speaking needs to be backed by character, but this is especially true in the case of those who admonish others and try to bring them to their sober senses.

2.4   "Apophthegmata Laconica" III, 235C–D:

While the games were being held at Olympia, an old man was desirous of seeing them, but could find no seat. As he went to place after place, he met with insults and jeers, and nobody made room for him. But when he came opposite the Spartans, all the boys and many of the men arose and yielded their places. Whereupon the assembled multitude of Greeks expressed their approbation of the custom by applause, and commended the action beyond measure; but the old man, shaking "his head grey-haired and grey-bearded," and with tears in his eyes, said, "Alas for the evil days! Because all the Greeks know what is right and fair, but the Spartans alone practice it."

To be sure, the Spartans are commended in the PS. But when one asks about the dominant motif, it is clearly that of the correction which the main character tearfully pronounces at the end. There is, of course, a profound moment in the utterance which surpasses the narrative occasion: knowing what is right and fair and practicing it represent the ideal human being *par excellence*!

2.5   "De Alexandri Magni Fortuna aut Virtute" IV, 331B:

Since he [Alexander] was the swiftest of foot of all the young men of his age, his comrades urged him to enter the Olympic games. He asked if the competitors were kings, and when his friends replied that they were not, he said that the contest was unfair, for it was one in which a victory would be over commoners, but a defeat would be the defeat of a king.

Alexander's comrades have considered only his athletic prowess. He, on the other hand, corrects this judgment by introducing the category of fairness— even if from a somewhat peculiar slant. Also noteworthy here is the absence of direct discourse in the correcting response.

2.6   "De Alexandri Magni Fortuna aut Virtute" IV, 331B–C:

When the thigh of his father Philip had been pierced by a spear in battle with the Triballians, and Philip, although he escaped with his life, was vexed with his lameness, Alexander said, "Be of good cheer, father, and go on your way rejoicing, that at each step you may recall your valour."

It is in the apparently lamentable circumstances of war's crippling blow to a healthy body that Alexander corrects the interpretation (the stimulus occasion for the response) that the inflicted lameness is an evil. To the contrary, it should be seen as a badge of courage and glory. Plutarch allows the PS to function as a credit to Alexander's nobility rather than attending to the reaction of Philip, as can be seen by the subsequent redactional application. Again, Plutarch has taken a rather straightforward correction PS (with commendation of Philip's valor as sub-motif) and turned it into something else when interpreting the story's point for the reader: it becomes a commendation of Alexander!

Are not these the words of a truly philosophic spirit which, because of its rapture for noble things, already revolts against mere physical encumbrances? How, then, think you, did he glory in his own wounds, remembering by each part of his body affected a nation overcome, a victory won, the capture of cities, the surrender of kings? He did not cover over nor hide his scars, but bore them with him openly as symbolic representations, graven on his body, of virtue and manly courage.

2.7   "De Alexandri Magni Fortuna aut Virtute" IV, 344F–345B:

Finally, the Macedonians routed the barbarians, and, when they had fallen, pulled down their city on their heads. But this was no help to Alexander; for he had been hurried from the field, arrow and all, and he had the shaft in his vitals; the arrow was as a bond or bolt holding his breastplate to his body. And when they tried forcibly to pull it out of the wound by the roots, as it were, the iron would not budge, since it was lodged in the bony part of the breast in front of the heart. They did not dare to saw off the protruding portion of the shaft, since they were afraid that the bone might be split by the jarring and cause excruciating pain, and that an internal haemorrhage might result. But when Alexander perceived their great perplexity and hesitation, he himself tried with his dagger to cut off the arrow close to his breastplate; but his hand was unsteady and affected by a torpid languor from the inflammation of the wound. Accordingly with encouraging words he urged those that were unwounded to take hold and not to be afraid; and he railed at some who were weeping and could not control themselves, others he branded as deserters, since they had not the courage to come to his assistance. And he cried aloud to his Companions, "Let no one be fainthearted even for my sake! For it will not be believed that I do not fear death, if you fear death for me!"

It is very difficult to tell how much of this rather detailed description of the scenario is Plutarch's paraphrase and how much belonged to the original correction PS (cf. 344C). The stimulus for the correcting response in direct discourse is clearly the paralysis of fear and consternation which seized all those about Alexander, who is too weak and shaken to do anything for himself in his injured state other than to correct those who are doing nothing. Unlike many stories, this one does not seem to have a hortatory purpose for the *reader*. The fact that the narrative ends with Alexander's pronouncement, without reporting whether the arrow was removed or whether Alexander survived, supports the view that this is a PS.

2.8   "De Garrulitate" VI, 508A–B:

But Fulvius, the friend of Caesar Augustus, heard the emperor, now an old man, lamenting the desolation of his house: two of his grandsons were dead, and Postumius, the only one surviving, was in exile because of some false accusation, and thus he was forced to import his wife's son into the imperial succession; yet he pitied his grandson and was planning to recall him from abroad. Fulvius divulged what he had heard to his own wife, and she to Livia; and Livia bitterly rebuked Caesar: if he had formed his design long ago, why did he not send for his grandson, instead of making her an object of enmity and strife to the successor to the empire. Accordingly, when Fulvius came to him in the morning, as was his custom, and said, "Hail, Caesar," Caesar replied, "Farewell, Fulvius." And Fulvius took his meaning and went away; going home at once, he sent for his wife, "Caesar has found out," he said, "that I have not kept his secret, and therefore I intend to kill myself." "It is right that you should," said his wife, "since, after living with me for so long a time, you have not learned to guard against my incontinent tongue. But let me die first." And, taking the sword, she dispatched herself before her husband.

This fascinating little story is especially interesting because of the question it raises for our study of PS. We have noted the presence of unusual narrative detail prior to the pronouncement in Plutarch's PS before. We have also noted the presence of direct discourse emphasis in the stimulus evoking the final response where we would ordinarily expect indirect discourse. This story commands attention because it moves to the concluding pronouncement with great force. The twist at the end, however, is that the correcting pronouncement—to our surprise—comes from someone other than the two "main" characters. One could ask if this is a PS at all. The final utterance of correction is so decisive for the whole account that it would be a mistake to deny it. This PS appears to be a Greek drama, tragic comedy, in miniature. It is difficult to imagine why Fulvius does not utter the closing pronouncement himself, since he must have known who betrayed him (by accident?). But part of his tragic flaw—and that which makes the final pronouncement all the more telling— is his naïve trust and blindness. The moment of truth is a masterpiece of PS denouement: one is genuinely undecided about the appropriate response; do you cry or laugh? Functionally, the first level of the concluding pronouncement is to correct Fulvius' stupidity: you were wrong to trust me to keep your secret, and a fool not to have known me better! As in other PS where the hortatory element is present, here in this tragedy the reader-listener is clearly warned: beware lest this happen to you! Plutarch himself uses it, moreover, to comment on a moral theme (here, talkativeness).

2.9   The following are additional examples of fairly straightforward correction PS: "Ad Principem Ineruditum" X, 779D; "De Vitando Aere Alieno" X, 831F; "Vitae Decem Oratorum: Isocrates" X, 838F–839A.

3.   Commendations

3.1   "De Alexandri Magni Fortuna aut Virtute" IV, 331E–332A:

But when he came to talk with Diogenes himself in Corinth, he was so awed and astounded with the life and the worth of the man that often, when remembrance of the philosopher came to him, he would say, "If I were not Alexander, I should be Diogenes."

To this is appended by Plutarch:

That is to say: "If I did not actively practise philosophy, I should apply myself to its theoretical pursuit." He did not say, "If I were not a king, I should be Diogenes," nor "If I were not rich and an Argead"; for he did not rank Fortune above Wisdom, nor a crown and royal purple above the philosopher's wallet and threadbare gown. But he said, "If I were not Alexander, I should be Diogenes"; that is to say: "If it were not my purpose to combine foreign things with things Greek, to traverse and civilize every continent, to search out the uttermost parts of land and sea, to push the bounds of Macedonia to the farthest Ocean, and to disseminate and shower the blessings of Greek justice and peace over every nation, I should not be content to sit quietly in the luxury of idle power, but I should emulate the frugality of Diogenes."

This commendation PS is particularly interesting because it demonstrates how Plutarch can take the original short form of the PS and enlarge upon it by continued use of the PS form itself. At some points Plutarch may be quoting variant traditions of the same story (cf. *Moralia* X, 782A; *Life of Alexander* XIV, 671D; see also Diogenes Laertius VI, 32; there are indirect references in Juvenal and Valerius Maximus), but the exchange regarding what Alexander did *not* say is clearly the redactional contribution of Plutarch. The original form of the story is a rather forthright recommendation of the person, life-style, and values of Diogenes, not of Alexander.

4.   Inquiries

4.1   "Vitae Decem Oratorum" X, 838F:

> When someone asked him [Isocrates] "What is oratory?" he said, "the art of making small things great and great things small."

Here the question-stimulus and the response stand in simple direct discourse. No narrative scene is necessary. The response places opposites into relationship with one another. The phrase is easily committed to memory and, in a sense, becomes a statement upon itself (brief but profound). A true orator has spoken!

4.2   "De Garrulitate" VI, 504A:

> And when a certain man at Athens was entertaining envoys from the king, at their earnest request he made every effort to gather the philosophers to meet them; and while the rest took part in the general conversation and made their contributions to it, but Zeno kept silent, the strangers, pledging him courteously, said, "And what are we to tell the king about you, Zeno?" "Nothing," said he, "except that there is an old man at Athens who can hold his tongue at a drinking-party."

The description of the setting is somewhat more detailed than usual, but this seems necessary to make the response to the question more witty or caustic. It is not altogether clear if there was a humorous intent, but it seems unlikely. A disapproving tone is unmistakable. This story qualifies as an inquiry-correction hybrid since the response not only answers the question of the strangers, thereby giving us important information about Zeno, but also shows Zeno's disapproval of the behavior of the other philosophers.

4.3   "Quomodo Adulator ab Amico Internoscatur" I, 50D:

> Surely there was no need to press the case against Melanthius, the parasite of Alexander of Pherae, who, in answer to those who asked how Alexander was slain, said, "By a stab through his ribs that hit me in my belly"; . . .

Here a witty response is given to a request for information. There may be a note of correction; the inquirers are mistaken if they think that their question has to do with Alexander alone. We may call it, therefore, a witty (perhaps correcting) inquiry.

4.4   "Apophthegmata Laconica" III, 230F:

> Pausanias, the son of Pleistoanax, in answer to the question why it was not permitted to change any of the ancient laws in their country, said, "Because the laws ought to have authority over the men, and not the men over the laws."

Here the main character is probably being put to the test through a question. The prior consideration of whether those laws may or may not be changed has been decided—it would seem—in the negative and now the question puts to the test the position of the speaker. The answer is accepted as a compelling defense and Pausanias is victor in the testing inquiry PS.

4.5   "Bellone an Pace Clariores Fuerint Athenienses" IV, 350D:

> But Isocrates, although he had declared that those who had risked their lives at Marathon had fought as though their souls were not their own, and although he had hymned their daring and their contempt of life, himself (so they say), when he was already an old man, replied to someone who asked him how he was getting on, "Even as does a man over ninety years of age who considers death the greatest of evils."

The response, which is prompted by a single inquiry, contains an unexpected element as the descriptive material has led the reader (along with the inquirer) to anticipate a view of death as glorious, not evil. Hence, there is a correcting quality to the response. Plutarch, for his part, is probably responsible for the correcting element. He then uses it toward the end of commending those who die in valiant defense of a nation and disapproving those who grow old extolling valor in words while themselves fearing "the clash of arms and the impact of phalanxes."

5.   Descriptions

5.1   "Quomodo Quis Suos in Virtute Sentiat Profectus" I, 79E:

> Aeschylus at the Isthmian games was watching a boxing-match, and when one of the men was hit the crowd in the theatre burst into a roar. Aeschylus nudged Ion of Chios, and said, "You see what a thing training is; the man who is hit says nothing; it is the spectators who shout."

and

> Brasidas caught a mouse among some dried figs, got bitten, and let it go; thereupon he said to himself, "Heavens, there is nothing so small or weak that it will not save its life if it has courage to defend itself."

In neither of these PS is there correcting, commending, objecting, inquiry, or questing going on. The pronouncement merely brings witty commentary to bear on the incident which has been briefly described. In the first story humor appears to be an end in itself, and Aeschylus is the skilled craftsman of humorous design. In the second a certain "truth" is at stake but not without a knowing smile!

6.   Quests

6.1   "De Pythiae Oraculis" V, 403F–404A:

> For this reason they usually appoint as priest rather old men. By exception, only a few years ago, a young man, not at all bad, but ambitious, who was in love with a girl, gained the office. At first he was able to control himself, and succeeded in keeping out of her way; but when she suddenly came in upon him as he was resting after drinking and dancing, he did the forbidden thing. Frightened and perturbed in consequence, he resorted at once to the oracle and asked the god about his sin, whether there were any way to obtain forgiveness or to expiate it; and he received this response: All things that must be doth the god condone.

This remarkable little story presents a complex but necessary narrative setting. It is taken for granted that the reader is familiar with the dynamics of the priestly vocation, the place of drinking and dancing (cult related?), what "the forbidden thing" is, and how this is interpreted in the priestly setting. The question posed to the oracle by the young priest is a genuine quest for forgiveness. The dominant "figure" qualified to respond to the quest is the oracular/divine word, the authoritative source of truth for the PS. Rather than the quester coming to the priest for judgment, it is the priest himself who turns to the higher source for judgment and release from his own error. The verdict is surprisingly mild. Such clear examples of quest PS are rare in the *Moralia*.

7.   Conclusions

7.1   This study of the PS in Plutarch's *Moralia* has shown the importance of an exacting standard of interrelationship between stimulus and response, narrative structure, and the kinds of tension and resolution which exist in the genre. Furthermore, with regard to the hortatory element it became apparent that the PS is normally concerned to broaden the base of appeal beyond the lauding of the hero type per se to include the person and conduct of the reader. Biographical interest, in fact, seems to be somewhat relative since Plutarch does not always honor this (cf. the Alexander PS) as redactor and the original form of the PS rarely—witty/caustic descriptions excepted—highlights this element in comparison with the ideal behavior or attitude which the key figure personifies. The hortatory element, be it expressed in approval, recommendation, and information or in disapproval, condemnation, and correction, is pervasive enough in virtually all of the PS to call it a nearly constant ingredient.

7.2   Since the hortatory element is so pervasive, one need not expand the classification grid to include another type, namely a "warning" or "strong admonition" type. Where the intensity of the recommended action or attitude is sufficiently pronounced, it merely serves as a special accent of composition. Virtually all of the PS—perhaps certain descriptions excepted—warn and admonish. It is probably because of their effectiveness in doing so that Plutarch is as thoroughly engaged by them as he is.

7.3   The longer one reads Plutarch the more one is impressed by his stature as ethicist, philosopher, theologian, teacher. The PS he has collected in the *Moralia* serve *his* compositional purposes. He can leave them in their original form if they serve those purposes—weaving them artfully into his overall discussion of virtue—and he can initiate a relatively small to a quite massive recasting when they do not. This freedom demonstrates Plutarch's positive valuation of the PS as a vehicle of educational communication. The examples above of Plutarch's appropriation of PS would be well worth multiplying into a full scale redactional study.

7.4   Comparison with the PS of the gospel tradition is a step to be taken with care and precision. The alloted space for this article prohibits a thoroughgoing confrontation. Focusing on the subject matter of the PS in this article in relation to the didactic sections of the gospel tradition—the value systems in conflict, the nature and source of virtue, etc.—one might draw up a number of possible connections. The problem, of course, is that not all of the New Testament references are going to share the PS form with their counterpart in the *Moralia*. The connections of subject matter, moreover, are frequently remote.

7.5   When a true PS parallel on both the level of subject matter and formal characteristics is studied, one also notes differences. Comparing 1.5 to Mark 2:15–17, we note that the objection is prompted by Jesus' acceptance of sinners, not by praise of the Spartans, and the categories of health and sickness are applied differently in the two stories. One could draw a parallel on the last point only by generalizing and making the social customs in the one case parallel to the divine norm for righteousness in the other. The specific content of each notwithstanding, the PS vehicle of communication functions in much the same way for each. Both groups of hearers are left to decide if they have heard the hortatory note in the final pronouncement or not. Further study of the PS in Plutarch's *Moralia* and the New Testament should prove interesting and beneficial for the reformulation of form critical categories in New Testament research.

WORKS CONSULTED

Plutarch
1960ff.   *Moralia.* 15 vols. With trans. by F. C. Babbitt et al. Loeb Classical
              Library. Cambridge, Mass.: Harvard University.

Ziegler, K.
1951   "Plutarchos von Chaironeia." Cols. 636–962 in *Paulys Realencyclo-
              pädie der classischen Altertumswissenschaft,* Band 21, 1.

Classifying Pronouncement Stories in Plutarch's *Parallel Lives*

Vernon K. Robbins

University of Illinois at Urbana-Champaign

ABSTRACT

Systematic analysis of the pronouncement stories in Plutarch's *Parallel Lives* has made it necessary to expand Tannehill's schema, which was developed on the basis of pronouncement stories in the Gospels. Using insights from David E. Aune's analysis of wisdom stories in Plutarch's essay on the *Banquet of the Seven Sages*, the pronouncement stories have been divided into three classes: (1) aphoristic, (2) adversative, and (3) affirmative pronouncement stories. The analysis gives examples of the types from the 200 pronouncement stories contained in Plutarch's *Lives* of *Alexander, Julius Caesar, Demosthenes,* and *Cicero*. The essay also indicates the frequency of the types in these *Lives* and interprets the frequency of the types in the context of the socio-political nature of Plutarch's *Parallel Lives*.

The two kinds of aphoristic pronouncement stories, the description and the inquiry, feature interaction by the primary character with ideas and situations rather than with people. The people are incidental to the setting.

The two basic types of adversative pronouncement stories, the correction and the dissent, feature an adversary relationship between the primary character and the secondary person or group. The correction features the primary character in the role of adversary in a setting where no one adopts an active role of counter-adversary to him. Since corrections may be directed toward first, second, or third persons, a distinction has been introduced between self-corrections (first person), direct corrections (second person), and indirect corrections (*to* a second person *about* a third person). There are two kinds of dissent stories, the objection and the rebuff. Both kinds feature secondary characters in an adversary relationship to the primary character. The objection features the primary character making the final, poignant statement in response to a dissenting statement, while the rebuff features a secondary character making the final, dissenting statement against the primary character.

The two basic types of affirmative pronouncement stories, the commendation and the laudation, feature the primary character and a secondary person or group in an affirming relationship rather than an adversary relationship as the story ends. In a commendation story, the primary character ends the story with a final statement of praise. Like the correction story, the commendation may occur in first person (self-commendation), second person (direct commendation), or third person (indirect commendation) form. In contrast to the commendation story, the laudation features a secondary person or group making a final statement of praise about the primary character in the *Life*.

The paper ends with a brief discussion of subtypes and hybrids within Plutarch's *Parallel Lives*.

0.1   Plutarch's *Lives* are a ready hunting ground for the analyst who seeks short narratives that end with pithy sayings or proverbs. The memorable sayings at the end of these stories exhibit the wit and wisdom of people in the midst of political and social life in Greece and Rome from the seventh century B.C. through the first century A.D. Plutarch's interest in short sayings in a brief narrative setting is evident from four documents entitled *Sayings (Apophthegms) of Kings and Commanders, Sayings (Apophthegms) of Romans, Sayings (Apophthegms) of Spartans*, and *Sayings (Apophthegms) of Spartan Women* that are attributed to him in the manuscript tradition /1/. In addition, portions of his *Lives* contain strings of apophthegms designed to display a special attribute of the person about whom the life is being written /2/. In Plutarch's *Alexander, Julius Caesar, Demosthenes*, and *Cicero* alone we have found approximately two-hundred narratives within the realm of ἀπόφθεγμα, παράδειγμα, ἀπομνημόνευμα, or χρεία that end with a brief, poignant saying. At the beginning of the *Alexander* (I.2), Plutarch describes the interests that guide him as he composes lives, and this description suggests the reason so many short narratives ending with brief sayings are present in them.

> I am not engaged in writing history (ἰστορίας), but lives (βίους). It is not in the most conspicuous of man's acts that good and bad qualities are necessarily best manifested. Some trivial act (πρᾶγμα βραχύ), a word (ῥῆμα), a jest (παιδιά) often shows up character far more than engagements, with thousands of dead, or pitched battles or blockades /3/.

This statement does not mean that Plutarch omits accounts of military engagements where 20,000 to 1 million of the enemy are left slain on the field /4/. But Plutarch is suggesting that little events, sayings, and remarks are a primary means by which he exhibits the character of the people about whom he is writing.

0.2   While the earliest investigation of brief literary units like those in Plutarch's *Lives* was produced by a classical scholar (Wartensleben, 1901), scholars of biblical, patristic, and rabbinic literature soon joined with another classical scholar (Gemoll, 1924) to produce a seven-year flurry of publications on them (Dibelius, 1919; Bultmann, 1921; Albertz, 1921; Bousset, 1923; Fascher, 1924; Fiebig, 1925). In the last part of the 1960's and the early part of the 1970's Fischel renewed the study of the brief literary units that accompany the portrayal of the sage in Mediterranean literature (1968, 1969, 1973), and Neusner (1970, 1971) produced a systematic analysis of brief literary units in rabbinic literature for the purpose of studying the traditions about the earliest rabbis. Then, within the last five years Tannehill (1975; 1980a; forthcoming) and Aune (1978), two New Testament scholars, have developed typological systems for studying these brief narratives within the literature of Mediterranean antiquity. The present study results from adaptation of the work of Aune and Tannehill to the study of brief narratives that end with terse, poignant sayings in Plutarch's *Lives*.

0.3   In accordance with the decision of the Pronouncement Story Work Group of the Society of Biblical Literature, I will refer to brief narratives that end with terse, poignant sayings as pronouncement stories /5/. Plutarch himself refers to these stories by various terms. Sometimes he refers to them as ἀποφθέγματα (apophthegms) or ἀπομνημονεύματα (remembrances or memorabilia), and frequently he uses both terms to refer to the same story, exhibiting a virtually synonymous usage of the two terms /6/. In at least one instance (*Antony* IV.3–4), Plutarch refers to a pronouncement story as a παράδειγμα (paradigm). In the scholarly investigation of stories such as these, Gemoll, Bousset, and Bultmann used the term apophthegm, Dibelius preferred the term paradigm, and Wartensleben and Fischel employed the term χρεία (chria), a term used in the second century *Progymnasmata* to refer to the brief stories the students were taught to compose in school. In this essay, "pronouncement story" is used as an overarching term to refer to brief literary units that contain two basic parts: (1) a situation and (2) a final utterance. In other words, the term pronouncement story refers to a literary unit that falls within the domain of apophthegm, remembrance, paradigm, or chria. Apophthegms that end with an action rather than a saying are not included. Also, remembrances, paradigms, or chriae that do not contain a final, poignant saying are not included. Pronouncement stories are all the instances of these forms that end with a memorable saying or remark. With the occurrence of a final saying in the story, a tensive relation exists between the first part of the story (the situation) and the final part of the story (the saying). In this investigation, the confrontational dynamics that arise out of the tension between the first and second parts call forth a typology which allows us to collect the stories into groups on the basis of formal similarities /7/. This grouping creates the potential for detailed, wholistic comparison of the stories in Plutarch's *Lives* with similar stories in other bodies of literature.

0.4   It has been necessary to limit the analysis to four of Plutarch's *Lives* during this stage of the research. Initial analysis of all fifty *Lives* is in progress, but only the *Lives* of *Alexander, Julius Caesar, Demosthenes*, and *Cicero* have been selected for this study. Since Plutarch wrote his *Lives* in pairs, this selection constitutes two pairs of *Lives* within the Plutarch corpus /8/. Analysis of the pronouncement stories in these *Lives* has produced a typology that divides the stories into three basic categories: (1) aphoristic pronouncement stories; (2) adversative pronouncement stories; and (3) affirmative pronouncement stories. Within these categories, specific types of pronouncement stories are differentiated on the basis of variations that exist in the context of confrontational dynamics.

1.   *The Aphoristic Pronouncement Story.* Some of the brief narratives that end in terse, poignant sayings in Plutarch's *Lives* feature interaction between the first and second parts of the story which can best be described as "aphoristic interaction." In an aphoristic pronouncement story, the first and second parts function as a rhetorical unit in which the primary character interacts with an idea in such a manner that the presence of other people in the setting is essentially coincidental /9/. Aphoristic tension in a pronouncement story is movement of thought induced by an aphorism (a statement of opinion: a saying, maxim, or proverb). Aphoristic interaction is interaction with thoughts and ideas in a context where there is no negative or positive interaction between people. The interaction between the primary character and the other characters in an aphoristic story is clever and perceptive rather than abrasive, judgmental, or commendatory. The presence of people with the primary character simply provides a context for the primary character to interact with the idea he addresses in the final utterance. The interaction, therefore, is friendly or neutral, because confrontation with ideas rather than people governs the dynamics. The primary character's interaction with the idea addressed in the final utterance takes precedence over his interaction with people either within the setting or outside of it.

1.1   *The Description.* Our analysis reveals two types of aphoristic pronouncement stories: (1) the description, and (2) the inquiry. The description is characterized by an absence of provocation in the situation and an absence of sarcasm, criticism, or commendation in the response. The primary character gives a perceptive or clever response to a situation, primarily on his own initiative, and describes, in his own inimitable manner, a situation or idea that arises out of the first part of the story.

1.11   A good example of a description in Plutarch's *Lives* exists in *Caesar* VII.3:

> The day for the election came, and as Caesar's mother accompanied him to the door in tears, he kissed her and said: "Mother, today thou shalt see thy son either pontifex maximus or an exile."

This story ends with a brief, poignant saying that provides a candid description of the situation by Caesar. Neither a negative nor a positive evaluation of Caesar's mother or the people of Rome dominates the story. Rather, Caesar displays his wisdom by means of a candid and perceptive balancing of the negative and positive dimensions of a political election. Also, nothing in the situation has required that Caesar respond. Rather, on his own initiative he chooses to display his perception of the situation.

1.12   Another description in Plutarch's *Lives* occurs just prior to the assassination of Caesar by Brutus. This story, in *Caesar* LXIII.7, portrays Caesar's confrontation with the event of death itself:

> Moreover, on the day before, when Marcus Lepidus was entertaining him at supper, Caesar chanced to be signing letters, as his custom was, while reclining at table, and the discourse turned suddenly to the subject of what sort of death was best; before anyone else could answer Caesar cried out: "That which is unexpected."

Again, this story ends with a memorable remark that arises out of the initiative of the primary character and contains neither a positive nor a negative evaluation of people in the setting or outside of it. The story is aphoristic, since Caesar's statement closes the rhetorical situation by delimiting the discussion with a brief remark that defines without correcting or commending any particular person. The story is a description rather than an inquiry, since even though a question has been asked in the first part of the story, the question has not been asked of Caesar himself. Instead, interrupting the deliberations of his host and the guests, Caesar interacts with the idea of death and describes the best way for it to occur.

1.13   Our analysis has uncovered only two stories in the four *Lives* that can be categorized as descriptions according to our criteria. These descriptions contain an utterance at the end that captures the import of a situation without commending or judging others. In other words, the situation is integrated with a memorable statement not by means of opposition or praise but by means of a saying or remark that emerges as the primary character describes a situation or idea on his own initiative. Once a person has read or heard such a story, the situation should call forth the utterance and the utterance should call forth the situation /10/.

1.14   The small number of descriptions in the four *Lives* indicates that political wisdom, as portrayed by Plutarch, is dominated by dynamics other than those which are simply gnomic, aphoristic, or proverbial. The descriptions that are present tend to emphasize the ability to perceive a political situation accurately or at least to describe it candidly. Sometimes, as in the story quoted from *Caesar* VII.3, the political wisdom displayed in descriptions is essentially prophetic. In other words, descriptions sometimes exhibit the ability of a political leader to perceive the potential positive or negative results that reside in a political situation. In the description stories, the political leader makes a brief, poignant statement that captures the dynamics of the situation without judging, correcting, or commending other people.

1.2   *The Inquiry.* The second type of aphoristic pronouncement story is the inquiry. This type is characterized by initiative on behalf of a friendly inquirer and by response to that inquiry in a cordial informative manner by the primary character (Tannehill, 1980b; forthcoming). In this type, the primary character responds with content designed to answer the inquiry on the basis of his particular possession of wit, perception, and skill with words. The response of the primary character is neither commendatory nor judgmental. Instead, the final utterance ends the story with a memorable remark in which the primary character interacts with a situation or an idea rather than with people.

1.21   A good example of an inquiry is found in Plutarch's *Sayings (Apophthegms) of Spartans* 215D (2):

> Being asked what form of instruction was most in vogue in Sparta, he [Agis] said, "Knowledge of how to rule and be ruled."

Another is present in *Sayings (Apophthegms) of Spartans* 224D (3):

> Being asked what freeborn boys had best learn, he [Leotychidas] said, "Those things which may help them when they become men."

Gemoll, in his famous study, considered this form to be the classic apophthegm (2). The form receives its two-part structure by means of a participial clause in the first part (ἐρωτηθείς . . .) and a third person finite verb in the second part (εἶπε or equivalent) /11/. Among the two-hundred pronouncement stories in the four *Lives*, seven clearly have this structure, and five more approximate this structure /12/. None of the stories with this structure in the four *Lives*, however, contains a response that is neither negative nor positive. Every story that contains initiative by an inquirer in the first part is characterized by interaction between the characters that introduces dynamics that are not simply aphoristic.

1.22   The absence of any aphoristic inquiry from Plutarch's *Alexander, Julius Caesar, Demosthenes*, and *Cicero* suggests that, from Plutarch's point of view, political leaders are rarely approached with open questions that attract candid, informative answers that contain neither positive nor negative overtones. The validity of this suggestion will need to be tested throughout the entire corpus. One should not be surprised, however, to find inquiries without positive or negative dynamics in a document like Diogenes Laertius' *Lives of Eminent Philosophers* (see Poulos: sect. 1). An example from Diogenes Laertius may serve as illustration:

> Once, when asked what is the best thing, he [Pittacus] replied, "To do well the work in hand." (1.77).

In this example, the primary character answers an inquiry in a philosophical rather than a political manner. For this reason, the questions are answered without commendation or correction. Philosophical wisdom is likely to manifest itself more regularly in direct, informative responses to open questions. In contrast, political wisdom manifests itself in contexts replete with conflict and counterplay. When a person confronts a political leader, he can expect a response that evaluates, praises, defends, or corrects.

1.23   In the four *Lives* of Plutarch analyzed in this study, therefore, only two stories have been found that fit the category of the aphoristic response. Both of these are descriptions rather than inquiries. It appears that the aphoristic pronouncement story is a more natural type to be found in the portrayal of philosophical wisdom than in the portrayal of political wisdom.

2.   *The Adversative Pronouncement Story*. In contrast to the small number of aphoristic pronouncement stories in the four *Lives*, a large number contain interaction that features alteration, reversal, or negation. These stories are "adversative" rather than aphoristic /13/. Our analysis suggests that there are two main types of adversative pronouncement stories: (1) the correction, and (2) the dissent. The dissent, in turn, can be divided into the objection and the rebuff.

2.1   *The Correction*. In a correction, the primary character gives a response, either on his own initiative or in reply to a question—a response that alters, reverses, or negates an assumption held by a person or group in the first part of the story (cf. Tannehill, 1980a: 146–147; 1980b; forthcoming). The type receives its name from the interaction between the characters in the first and second parts of the story. In a correction, there is no criticism of the primary character either before or after the statement by him. Rather, the primary character adopts the position of an adversary, either gently or aggressively, without being treated as an adversary by others in the story. The end result of the story is the presence of adversative tension initiated by the primary character that calls for continued reflection. Should the final pronouncement be accepted as an authoritative truth, or was the primary aim of the statement to challenge the person in the story to re-examine his presuppositions? Also, did the party or group to which the primary character responded accept or reject the point of view presented by the primary character? The story gives little or no clue to resolve these issues. Rather, alteration, negation, or reversal is initiated by the primary character in a context where no one criticizes him either before or after his statement.

2.11   Since the interaction between the characters is central in the correction story rather than coincidental, as in the description and the inquiry, it is necessary to differentiate the three basic ways in which corrective interaction may occur in a narrative context. The primary character may interact with himself, may interact directly with a second person, or may interact with a third person. In other words, personal interaction occurs in first, second, or third person contexts. Therefore, a correction may be a self-correction, a direct correction (of a second person), or an indirect correction (to a second person about a third person) /14/.

2.12   *The Self-Correction*. Self-corrections feature the primary character correcting himself either in public or in private. An example of a self-correction in public is present in *Alexander* LVIII.6:

> And at another time, when his Macedonians hesitated to advance upon the citadel called Nysa because there was a deep river in front of it, Alexander, halting on the

bank, cried: "Most miserable man that I am, why, pray, have I not learned to swim?" and at once, carrying his shield, he would have tried to cross.

In this story, Alexander interacts with himself in an adversative, corrective manner. He becomes his own adversary when he openly states that his failure to learn to swim now opposes his desire to swim.

2.121   In contrast to the public setting for the Alexander story, the setting is private in the self-correction in *Caesar* XLV.7–8:

> When Pompey, on the other wing, saw his horsemen scattered in flight, he was no longer the same man, nor remembered that he was Pompey the Great, but more like one whom Heaven has robbed of his wits than anything else, he went off without a word to his tent, sat down there, and awaited what was to come, until his forces were all routed and the enemy were assailing his ramparts and fighting with their defenders. Then he came to his senses, as it were, and with this one ejaculation, as they say, "What, even to my quarters?" took off his fighting and general's dress, put on one suitable for a fugitive, and stole away.

In this story the final remark is less obviously a self-correction since the remark is only part of Pompey's response to the situation. The complete response of Pompey includes both a remark and an action. By means of the remark and the action, Pompey corrects himself in a situation in which he is about to be in danger by lack of appropriate action. In this story no one but the reader and Pompey himself can hear the remark and see the action by which the primary character responds to the situation. Whether in public or in private, the self-correction features the primary character as his own adversary. The primary character creates corrective tension with himself in the response that ends the story.

2.13   *The Direct Correction.* While only a few self-corrections exist in the four *Lives*, approximately fifty-five of the pronouncement stories are direct corrections. The direct correction features the primary character responding directly to a person or group with a statement that alters, reverses, or negates an assumption held by that person or group. In some direct corrections, a person may actually state the point of view that is corrected by the primary character, as in *Cicero* XXV.4:

> And when Crassus expressed his satisfaction with the Stoics because they represented the good man as rich, "Consider," said Cicero, "whether your satisfaction is not rather due to their declaration that all things belong to the wise."

In this story, the statement by Crassus is corrected by the primary character (Cicero) in the final statement. The alteration of Crassus' point of view is signaled by the opening words of Cicero's statement: ὅρα μὴ μᾶλλον ("consider . . . whether your satisfaction is not rather"). Cicero challenges Crassus' presupposition that he is concerned about goodness. Rather, Cicero affirms, Crassus is more concerned about being wise enough to accumulate all the things he covets. In other words, since Crassus has stated his point of view in the first part of the story, the response by Cicero is able to make a subtle play on goodness vs. wisdom and wealth vs. the desire to possess all things. The final statement by Cicero corrects Crassus' faulty view of himself as a person who is attracted to goodness. Rather, Cicero asserts, Crassus is simply interested in being smart enough to attain all the possessions he desires. In other direct corrections, the assumption of the person or group is not stated in the first part but becomes obvious in the final statement, as in *Alexander* XXVIII.3:

> When he had been hit by an arrow and was suffering great pain, he said: "This, my friends, that flows here, is blood, and not 'Ichor, such as flows from the veins of the blessed gods.'"

The final saying makes it clear that his friends are entertaining the possibility that Alexander is divine. The presupposition among his friends creates the situation in which Alexander responds with a corrective statement when he has been wounded by an arrow.

Whether or not the presupposition is explicitly stated by the person or group, the direct correction shows people in face to face confrontation. In the direct correction, the primary character adopts the role of an adversary who corrects the person or group to whom he is speaking. Neither before nor after the response of the primary character, however, does the person or group adopt the role of an adversary of the primary character.

2.14   *The Indirect Correction.* In one-third of the correction stories (28 out of 85) in the four *Lives*, the primary character makes a corrective utterance about a third party or group rather than making a corrective utterance directly to a second party. This kind of adversative pronouncement story is an indirect correction. In an indirect correction, the primary character alters, negates, or reverses a statement made or a presupposition held by a third party. In other words, instead of adopting the role of adversary by directly confronting the person or group, the primary character corrects a third party or group by making a statement about them. An example of an indirect correction is found in *Cicero* XXVI.3:

> Again, after hearing that Vatinius was dead, and then after a little learning for a surety that he was alive, "Wretchedly perish, then," said Cicero, "the wretch who lied!"

This story contains a corrective final saying in which Cicero adopts the role of adversary to the one who spread the rumor that Vatinius had died. The statement also manifests Cicero's adoption of the role of adversary against Vatinius. The story is an indirect correction rather than a direct correction, because Cicero makes his statement *about* the people rather than *to* them.

Occasionally the primary character may ask a question and give an answer in an indirect correction. In *Caesar* LXII.9, for example, Caesar creates the setting of an indirect correction by asking about Cassius and answering his own question with a memorable remark:

Moreover, Caesar actually suspected him [Cassius], so that he once said to his friends: "What, think ye, doth Cassius want? I like him not over much, for he is much too pale."

In an indirect correction, the person who is corrected is usually not present in the setting. The primary character may therefore, as in this instance, initiate the adversative tension by means of a question that provides the setting for an adversative remark that concludes the story.

2.15   Approximately forty-three percent (85 out of 200) of the pronouncement stories in the four *Lives* analyzed in this study are adversative stories of the correction type. Correction stories feature primary characters teaching others how to think and act in a setting where no one shows any opposition to the speaker. This type of story, therefore, may function didactically in contexts where little or no socio-political conflict is present. On the other hand, the presence of over eighty correction stories correlates well with Plutarch's assertion that he is interested in teaching the reader about good and bad character by means of the "trivial acts, words, and jests" he includes in the narrative. The large number of correction stories in the *Lives* shows how the didactic purpose of the narrative is reflected in the little episodes that exhibit the responses of various people to one another. On the other hand, approximately thirty-three percent of the correction stories are indirect rather than direct corrections. The presence of this many indirect corrections in Plutarch's *Lives* may be important, since it appears that the curt, negative remarks about other people in the indirect corrections are rather weak didactic instruments. In other words, the indirect corrections tend to exhibit general disapproval rather than substantive correction. For this reason, they carry very little didactic freight in the narrative. If one subtracts the indirect corrections from the correction stories, only twenty-eight percent (55 out of 200) of the pronouncement stories in the four *Lives* have a strong didactic function in contexts relatively free from socio-political conflict. This observation may be important in relation to other literature. If the wisdom being taught in the narrative were philosophical rather than socio-political, one might expect as high as seventy-five to eighty percent of the pronouncement stories to be constituted by descriptions, inquiries, and corrections /15/. In other words, by means of interaction directly with ideas and general situations (aphoristic pronouncement stories) and by means of initiative with people who hold misconceptions (correction stories), the author may present a basic system of understanding to the reader by means of a philosopher-teacher's involvement in teaching and correction. Since virtually no pronouncement stories in the fifty *Lives* of Plutarch are aphoristic, and only twenty-eight percent of the pronouncement stories in these four *Lives* are direct corrections, a relatively small portion of the pronouncement stories function as didactic instruments free from socio-political conflict.

Only a few (approximately two or three percent) of the correction stories are self-corrections. Yet the presence of any such stories is important. One of the attributes of a wise political leader is the ability to enter into self-criticism. In contrast, religious leaders virtually never enter into public self-criticism, and Socrates appears to be unique among philosophers for his persistent self-critical stance in public (as portrayed by Plato). The presence or absence of self-corrections in various bodies of literature may reveal relationships or distinctions between various socio-political, socio-religious, and socio-philosophical arenas of life in Mediterranean culture.

2.2   The Dissent. The other basic type of adversative pronouncement story features a person or group in an active role of adversary to the primary character. Since these stories portray dissension by a person or group against the primary character, they are dissent stories. We have found two kinds of dissent stories in the four *Lives* of Plutarch: (a) the objection and (b) the rebuff.

2.21   The Objection. The objection story features the primary character uttering the final, poignant saying in response to dissent by a secondary party or group (Tannehill, 1980a: 145–146; forthcoming). In this kind of dissent story, a person or group adopts the role of adversary by objecting to the primary character in a situation that calls forth a response by the primary character. The adversative tension in an objection is characterized by the active adversary role of the secondary party or group to which the primary character responds in the final saying.

2.211 In some examples of the objection, a saying in the first part of the story provides the opportunity for a response that wittily turns the objection back upon the objector. An example is present in *Demosthenes* VIII.3–5:

> Demosthenes was rarely heard to speak on the spur of the moment, but though the people often called upon him by name as he sat in the assembly, he would not come forward unless he had given thought to the question and was prepared to speak upon it. For this, many of the popular leaders used to rail at him, and Pytheas, in particular, once told him scoffingly that his arguments smelt of lamp-wicks. To him, then, Demosthenes made a sharp answer. "Indeed," said he, "thy lamp and mine, O Pytheas, are not privy to the same pursuits."

Sometimes, instead, the final saying refers to something that was told to the reader in the narrational framework of the first part. *Cicero* VII.8 is an example:

> And again, the orator Hortensius did not venture to plead the cause of Verres directly, but was persuaded to appear for him at the assessment of the fine, and received an ivory sphinx as his reward; and when Cicero made some oblique reference to him and Hortensius declared that he had no skill in solving riddles, "And yet," said Cicero, "thou hast the Sphinx at thy house."

In this story, the subject matter of the final saying turns an item from the narrational framework ("and received an ivory sphinx as his reward") back upon the objector. In other words, the unity of this objection story derives not from rewording the objector's statement but from a response that makes a play on a dimension introduced by means of narrative comment. In other examples an objection may be voiced by means of a question, as in *Caesar* X.8–9:

> Caesar divorced Pompeia at once, but when he was summoned to testify at the trial, he said he knew nothing about the matters with which Clodius was charged. His statement appeared strange, and the prosecutor therefore asked, "Why, then, didst thou divorce thy wife?" "Because," said Caesar, "I thought my wife ought not even be under suspicion."

In this story the objection to Caesar's explanation is couched in a question. Caesar responds directly to this question with the saying that concludes the story. Sometimes, though the objection is addressed to the primary character, it is not certain that the primary character responds directly to those who objected. The objection story in *Alexander* XLI.1–2 leaves this kind of uncertainty concerning the audience of the final saying:

> Alexander, then, in exercising himself and at the same time inciting others to deeds of valour, was wont to court danger; but his friends, whose wealth and magnificence now gave them a desire to live in luxury and idleness, were impatient of his long wanderings and military expeditions, and gradually went so far as to abuse him and speak ill of him. He, however, was very mildly disposed at first toward this treatment of himself, and used to say that it was the lot of a king to confer favours and be ill-spoken of therefor.

In this story Alexander responds to the objections that his wanderings and expeditions were too extensive. It is not certain that he spoke directly back to those who objected to him. It appears that he responded in a less confrontational manner to the adversative comments of his friends.

2.22   *The Rebuff.* As in the objection story, so in the rebuff story a secondary party or group adopts the role of adversary to the primary character. In contrast to the objection where the dissent occurs in the first part of the story, the rebuff features the dissent in a final, poignant response by a secondary character. In other words, the primary character of the writing does not make the final, poignant statement in the rebuff story. Instead, a statement or action of the primary character stimulates a response by a secondary character who utters a final, dissenting statement that ends the story. In the rebuff, therefore, the adversative tension reaches its climax in a statement by a person other than the primary character of the writing. An example of a rebuff is found in *Alexander* LVIII.7–9:

> And when, after he [Alexander] had put a stop to the fighting, ambassadors came from the beleaguered cities to beg for terms, they were amazed, to begin with, to see him in full armour and without an attendant; and besides, when a cushion was

brought him for his use, he ordered the eldest of the ambassadors, Acuphis by name, to take it for his seat. Acuphis, accordingly, astonished at his magnanimity and courtesy, asked what he wished them to do in order to be his friends. "Thy countrymen," said Alexander, "must make thee ruler, and send me a hundred of their best men." At this Acuphis laughed, and said: "Nay, O King, I shall rule better if I send to thee the worst men rather than the best."

In this story, the secondary character ends with a statement that negates and alters the statement of the primary character, Alexander. In the story, Alexander does not respond to the dissent voiced by Acuphis. Therefore, this story is a rebuff story rather than an objection. Another rebuff story is found in *Caesar* LXIII.5–6:

A certain seer warned Caesar to be on his guard against a great peril on the day of the month of March which the Romans call the Ides; and when the day had come and Caesar was on his way to the senate-house, he greeted the seer with a jest and said: "Well, the Ides of March are come," and the seer said to him softly: "Aye, they are come, but they are not gone."

In this story again, the subject of the *Life*, Caesar, is not allowed the final response. The statement of the primary character, Caesar, calls forth a final, dissenting statement by the secondary character, the seer. In the rebuff, the tables are turned on the primary character. The wit and wisdom of a person other than the primary character carries the day, leaving the primary character speechless.

2.23   There are twenty-five rebuff stories and thirty objection stories in the four *Lives* analyzed in this study. In other words, twenty-eight percent of all the pronouncement stories in the four *Lives* are dissent stories (55 out of 200), while only one percent of the stories are aphoristic. In order to maintain a total perspective, we must remain aware that forty-three percent of the pronouncement stories are corrections. However, the correction appears to be the most common type of pronouncement story in much Graeco-Roman literature /16/. Corrections seem to reflect the didactic nature of Mediterranean literature. Therefore, the number of dissent stories vis-à-vis aphoristic pronouncement stories may reveal a more significant dimension of the literature than the number of correction stories. The more controversial, or in other terms, the more socio-politically electric the teaching is, the more dissent stories one may expect to find within the narrative. Since dissent stories in the *Lives* of Plutarch outnumber aphoristic stories fifty-five to two, it is obvious that Plutarch's *Lives* are significantly infused with interaction that is socio-politically alive.

It is remarkable that there are almost as many rebuff stories (25) as objection stories (30) in these four *Lives*. It appears that rebuff stories are virtually non-existent in literature where the primary character is a religious leader. In the portrayal of a religious leader, the primary character in the narrative issues the final, poignant statement. Therefore, religious literature may contain many objection stories but few or no rebuff stories. In contrast, one of the attributes of a political leader, so far as Plutarch is concerned, is the ability to accept a rebuff when the other person has shown admirable wit or wisdom. For this reason, Alexander and Caesar accept a rebuff when they know they have been outwitted, at least for the moment.

Adversative pronouncement stories constitute a significant group among the stories that end with terse, poignant sayings in Plutarch's *Lives*. In fact, seventy percent of the pronouncement stories in the four *Lives* of Plutarch are adversative pronouncement stories. Sixty percent of the adversative stories are correction stories that feature the primary character adopting an adversary role in a context where no other person or group adopts an active role as counter-adversary. Among the correction stories are a few self-corrections where the primary character applies criticism to himself. Forty percent of the adversative stories are dissent stories that feature a primary character in a setting where an adversary role is actively adopted by a secondary person or group. These dissent stories display the socio-political dynamics of Plutarch's *Lives* where people adopt active adversary roles against the primary character in the narrative. Among the dissent stories are rebuffs where the primary character does not attempt to respond to statements of dissent that contain admirable wit or wisdom. Like the self-corrections, the rebuff stories indicate that political wisdom may require restraint or reversal of one's point of view on the basis of experience in the socio-political arena.

3.   *The Affirmative Pronouncement Story.* In addition to a large number of adversative pronouncement stories, the four *Lives* investigated in this study contain a significant number of affirmative pronouncement stories. Affirmative pronouncement stories may or may not contain adversative dynamics, but the final response releases the tension by means of agreement or praise. Our analysis suggests two types of affirmative pronouncement stories: (1) the commendation, and (2) the laudation.

3.1   *The Commendation.* The commendation story features the primary character adopting an affirming role rather than an adversary role. The final saying in a commendation features the primary character affirming some aspect of another person or group. Like the correction story, the commendation story occurs in a setting in which first, second, or third person confrontation may be present. Therefore, a commendation story may be a self-commendation (first person), a direct commendation (second person), or an indirect commendation (third person).

3.11   *The Self-Commendation.* One of the most famous self-commendation stories exists in *Caesar* L.1-3:

> On leaving that country and traversing Asia, he learned that Domitius had been defeated by Pharnaces the son of Mithridates and had fled from Pontus with a few followers; also that Pharnaces, using his victory without stint, and occupying

Bithynia and Cappadocia, was aiming to secure the country called Lesser Armenia, and was rousing to revolt all the princes and tetrarchs there. At once, therefore, Caesar marched against him with three legions, fought a great battle with him near the city of Zela, drove him in flight out of Pontus, and annihilated his army. In announcing the swiftness and fierceness of this battle to one of his friends at Rome, Amantius, Caesar wrote three words, "I came, I saw, I conquered."

In this story, Caesar recounts his successful military endeavors in the form of self-commendation. Likewise, Cicero describes his return from exile in the form of a self-commendation in *Cicero* XXXIII.7:

Thus Cicero came home in the sixteenth month after his exile; and so great was the joy of the cities and the eagerness of men to meet him that what was said by Cicero afterwards fell short of the truth. He said, namely, that Italy had taken him on her shoulders and carried him into Rome.

Again, this story recounts an event in the past, in a form in which the primary character directs praise toward himself. Sometimes the rehearsal of a past event in a self-commendation produces lengthy, detailed narration. The self-commendation of *Alexander* LX.1–6 is an example:

Of his campaign against Porus he himself [Alexander] has given an account in his letters. He says, namely, that the river Hydaspes flowed between the two camps, and that Porus stationed his elephants on the opposite bank and kept continual watch of the crossing. He himself, accordingly, day by day caused a great din and tumult to be made in his camp, and thereby accustomed the Barbarians not to be alarmed. Then, on a dark and stormy night, he took a part of his infantry and the best of his horsemen, and after proceeding along the river to a distance from where the enemy lay, crossed over to a small island. Here rain fell in torrents, and many tornadoes and thunderbolts dashed down upon his men; but nevertheless, although he saw that many of them were being burned to death by the thunderbolts, he set out from the islet and made for the opposite banks. But the Hydaspes, made violent by the storm and dashing high against its bank, made a great breach in it, and a large part of the stream was setting in that direction; and the shore between the two currents gave his men no sure footing, since it was broken and slippery. And here it was that he is said to have cried: "O Athenians, can ye possibly believe what perils I am undergoing to win glory in your eyes?"

In the midst of storm and frustration, Alexander exercises a moment of wit as he publicly praises himself for his willingness to cope with such miserable circumstances.

The presence of self-commendations in Plutarch's *Lives* is highly interesting in light of Plutarch's essay *On Self-Praise*. Plutarch suggests that there are circumstances in which self-praise is acceptable or even recommendable in spite of common agreement that self-praise is to be rejected (see Betz). In Plutarch's *Lives*, self-praise by Greek leaders is usually appropriate and moderated by an insistence by the primary character that he is not divine. In contrast, some of the Roman leaders launch into self-praise that reflects badly on their character.

3.12   *The Direct Commendation.* In contrast to adversative stories, where the direct correction represents the largest number of the group, less than five direct commendations exist in these four *Lives*. In the direct commendation, the final saying presents the sage praising a person whose action or statement has been featured in the first part of the story. *Alexander* XXXIX.3 is an example of this kind of story:

> Again, a common Macedonian was driving a mule laden with some of the royal gold, and when the beast gave out, took the load on his own shoulders and tried to carry it. The king, then, seeing the man in great distress and learning the facts of the case, said, as the man was about to lay his burden down, "Don't give out, but finish your journey by taking this load to your own tent."

In this story, Alexander commends a common Macedonian by rewarding him with the load of gold which he struggled to carry for Alexander.

3.13   *The Indirect Commendation.* Approximately ten indirect commendations exist in the four *Lives*. In an indirect commendation the primary character does not confront the person who is being commended. An example of the indirect commendation is found in *Alexander* VIII.4:

> Aristotle he [Alexander] admired at the first, and loved him, as he himself used to say, more than he did his father, for that the one had given him life, but the other had taught him a noble life.

Another is found in *Alexander* XV.8:

> Furthermore, the gravestone of Achilles he [Alexander] anointed with oil, ran a race by it with his companions, naked, as is the custom, and then crowned it with garlands, pronouncing the hero happy in having, while he lived, a faithful friend, and after death, a great herald of his fame.

Some commendation stories are extremely brief, like the one found in *Cicero* XXIV.6:

> And when he [Cicero] was asked which of the speeches of Demosthenes he thought the best, he replied, "the longest."

3.14   Among commendation stories, the majority are either self-commendations or indirect commendations. Rarely in a *Life* of Plutarch does the primary character commend a person in a setting of direct confrontation. Rather, he either commends himself or commends prestigious people, either dead or alive, who are not present in the setting.

3.2   *The Laudation.* The other basic kind of affirmative pronouncement story is the laudation. In a laudation story, a person other than the subject of the *Life* ends the story with a statement that praises the subject of the *Life*. There are eighteen laudations in these four *Lives*. *Alexander* III.8–9 is an example:

> To Philip, however, who had just taken Potidaea, there came three messages at the same time: the first that Parmenio had conquered the Illyrians in a great battle, the second that his race-horse had won a victory at the Olympic games, while a third announced the birth of Alexander. These things delighted him, of course, and the

seers raised his spirits still higher by declaring that the son whose birth coincided with three victories would be always victorious.

In this story, seers laud Alexander as one who will achieve great success in military exploits. Neither Philip, who is featured in the story, nor Alexander, who is the subject of the *Life*, issues the affirmation of Alexander's greatness. Rather, other people laud Alexander as one who will be great beyond ordinary measures.

3.21   Another laudation occurs in *Cicero* XXII.5–6, midway in the *Life* after Cicero has triumphed over Catiline and his fellow-conspirators:

> It was now evening, and Cicero went up through the forum to his house, the citizens no longer escorting him on his way with silent decorum, but receiving him with cries and clapping of hands as he passed along, calling him the saviour and founder of his country. And many lights illuminated the streets, since people placed lamps and torches at their doors. The women, too, displayed lights upon the housetops in honour of the man, and that they might see him going up to his home in great state under escort of the noblest citizens. Most of these had brought to an end great wars and entered the city in triumph, and had added to the Roman dominion no small extent of land and sea; but they now walked along confessing to one another that to many of the commanders and generals of the time the Roman people were indebted for wealth and spoils and power, but for preservation and safety to Cicero alone, who had freed them from so peculiar and so great a peril.

This story again features people other than the subject of the Life issuing the final, poignant statement that brings the story to its climax. It is a laudation of the subject of the *Life* by secondary characters.

3.22   Both commendations and laudations display affirmative expression in the pronouncement story. Commendations feature the primary character praising himself, praising another person in face-to-face confrontation, or praising a person who is not present in the setting. Therefore, commendations, like corrections, occur in self (first person), direct (second person), or indirect (third person) forms. In addition, the affirmative pronouncement story may occur in the form of a laudation. The laudation, like the rebuff, features a person other than the primary character of the *Life* stating the final, poignant response.

4.   *Special Forms in Plutarch's Parallel Lives.* Any classification system will leave important phenomena unattended. For this reason it is necessary to devise a means to give appropriate attention to material not directly addressed by the schema. We suggest a distinction between subtypes and hybrids in order to analyze dimensions of pronouncement stories that are not highlighted by the confrontational schema introduced thus far.

4.1   *Subtypes of Pronouncement Stories.* Many features cut across the boundaries of the types analyzed in this paper. For example, many of the stories are humorous, others feature proverbial sayings, and still others use quotations from Homer or the tragedians within the final, poignant saying. These stories are subtypes in the classification system presented in this paper. An investigator may wish to analyze all the humorous pronouncement stories in Plutarch's *Lives*. Such a project would concern itself with humorous descriptions, humorous corrections, humorous objections, etc. This project would be a study of a particular subtype of pronouncement story in Plutarch's *Lives*. The presence or absence of humor within certain types may be informative. For example, all the self-corrections may be humorous over against the self-commendations, which may contain no humor. In the comparison of certain bodies of literature, or in the comparison of *Lives* of Plutarch with one another, such observations may lead to informative conclusions.

4.11   Paradigmatic pronouncement stories constitute a major subtype within Plutarch's *Lives*. Aune considered the wisdom story that exhibited the wisdom of the sage by means of practical action or conduct to be so important that he developed a special category (the paradigmatic wisdom story) to highlight it (Aune: 66–67). Our analysis suggests that, on the one hand, paradigmatic actions occur in almost every type of pronouncement story. Such stories are a subtype (including paradigmatic corrections, paradigmatic objections, etc.) that deserves special investigation. On the other hand, stories other than pronouncement stories contain this feature. This should cause no surprise. As soon as a person begins to examine subtypes, one should expect to find the special feature (like humor, proverbs, quotations from prestigious literature, or paradigmatic actions) in various forms and contexts throughout the work.

4.2   *Hybrid Pronouncement Stories.* Within any body of literature, a particular combination of several confrontational dynamics may characterize a significant number of pronouncement stories. At least one such group exists in Plutarch's *Lives*. A number of stories are self-defense stories. These stories combine either self-commendation or self-correction with direct or indirect correction. Such a combination produces a hybrid type within the confrontational classification system presented in this essay.

4.21   An example of a self-defense story is present in *Caesar* XLVI.1:

> But Caesar, when he reached Pompey's ramparts and saw those of the enemy who were already lying dead there and those who were still falling, said with a groan: "They would have it so; they brought me to such a pass that if I, Gaius Caesar, after waging successfully the greatest wars, had dismissed my forces, I should have been condemned in their courts."

This story combines self-commendation with indirect correction. Caesar commends himself for overcoming a military assault by Pompey that would have completely destroyed his (Caesar's) position of power. Also, Caesar corrects Pompey's forces for having created a situation in which it was necessary for the opposition to undertake armed violence against them. This story is therefore a self-defense which combines self-commendation with indirect correction.

4.22   Another self-defense story is found in *Alexander* XXII.4–5:

> Furthermore, on learning that Damon and Timotheus, two Macedonian soldiers under Parmenio's command, had ruined the wives of certain mercenaries, he wrote to Parmenio ordering him, in case the men were convicted, to punish them and put them to death as wild beasts born for the destruction of mankind. In this letter he also wrote expressly concerning himself: "As for me, indeed, it will be found not only that I have not seen the wife of Dareius or desired to see her, but that I have not even allowed people to speak to me of her beauty."

This story combines self-commendation with direct correction. Alexander commends himself for his exemplary self-restraint in regards to Dareius' wife. Also, his response corrects the assumption (which he suspects that Parmenio may have) that he himself probably compelled Dareius' wife to have sexual relations with him.

5.   *Conclusion.* This essay could not include discussion of the systems developed by Tannehill and Aune because it is necessary to use the space to display examples of the forms in Plutarch's *Lives*. Also, this essay could not examine philological data that provide the syntactical unity and the confrontational dynamics in the stories. Moreover, there was not space to compare various *Lives* with one another or with other literature like Diogenes Laertius' *Lives of Eminent Philosophers* or the Gospels.

5.1   The purpose of this essay has been to expand and adapt the classification systems developed by Tannehill and Aune to bring the extensive variety of the pronouncement stories in Plutarch's *Parallel Lives* into purview. On the one hand, Aune's analysis of the stories in Plutarch's *Banquet of the Seven Sages* suggested the necessity for discovering the overall classes of pronouncement stories in the corpus. Adapting and expanding his categories of gnomic and agonistic wisdom stories (Aune: 66), we have developed three basic categories: (a) aphoristic, (b) adversative, and (c) affirmative pronouncement stories. These three classes appear to account for the basic kinds of dynamics that arise in pronouncement stories. Within the context of these three classes of pronouncement stories, we have adapted and expanded the typology of Tannehill to include adversative and affirmative interaction through a final, poignant statement by someone other than the primary character in the *Life*. The rebuff story and the laudation story, two forms not mentioned by Tannehill or Aune, emerged from this analysis. Also, we expanded the analysis to allow differentiation between first, second, and third person confrontational dynamics. This analysis produced a distinction between the self, direct, and indirect forms of the correction and the commendation.

5.2   The overall purpose of this essay has been to develop a classification system extensive enough to allow comparison of the most disparate
kinds of pronouncement stories within Mediterranean literature. The variety
within the two hundred stories selected for this study suggests that Aune's
categories are too broad to offer a satisfying system for comparing various
bodies of literature within the Mediterranean world. Also, it calls for finer
tuning than that which exists in Tannehill's system, which was developed on
the basis of pronouncement stories in the Gospels. The programmatic form
of the essay, however, has not permitted discussion of the perceptive analysis
of the "acclamation" and the "false solution" by Aune (66), nor has it allowed discussion of Tannehill's analysis of tensive language in sayings and
stories in the Synoptic Gospels (1980a). Perhaps, however, the classification
system introduced here can stimulate detailed comparison of bodies of literature on the basis of the short narratives in them that end with terse, poignant sayings /17/.

NOTES

/1/   There has been considerable debate whether these documents were actually written by
Plutarch or by someone highly interested in Plutarch's *Lives*. The overlap between the stories in
these collections and the stories in the *Lives* has led to suggestions that someone other than
Plutarch excerpted them from the *Lives*. Others have suggested that Plutarch made these col-
lections and drew on them as he wrote his *Lives*. See the introduction by F. C. Babbitt in
Plutarch's Moralia, vol. III (Cambridge: Harvard University, 1968) 3–7 and Ziegler: 863–867.

/2/   E.g., *Cicero* XXV–XXVII, XXXVIII; *Demosthenes* X–XI; *Alexander* XXXIX–XL;
Marcus Cato VIII–IX; *Lycurgus* XIX–XX; *Phocion* XXIII–XXIV.

/3/   This translation is from Barrow (53). Unless otherwise indicated, the translations are
based on the English text in *Plutarch's Lives*, trans. Bernadotte Perrin (LCL VII; Cambridge:
Harvard University, 1971), with modifications when an expression has obscured features in the
Greek text important for the appropriate classification of the unit. The paragraph numbers
refer to the Teubner and the newer LCL editions. The numbers in parentheses refer to the
older LCL editions. The two quotations from Plutarch's *Sayings of Spartans* are taken from
Plutarch's Moralia, trans. Frank C. Babbitt (LCL III; Cambridge: Harvard University, 1968).

/4/   Cf. *Alexander* XVI.15 (7); XXXIII.6–8 (4–5); *Caesar* XV.5 (3); XIX.11–12 (5); XX.5
(3); XXII.5 (3).

/5/   At the present time, I prefer the name "gnomic chria" to describe these literary units,
because I think the name locates the form in the context of terms used in ancient literature.

/6/   See *Lycurgus* 19.3–4; 20.1–6; *Themistocles* 18.2–5; *Marcus Cato* 8.1–9.7; *Brutus* 2.6–8
(4–5). Cf. the remarks by Spencer (14).

/7/   Two examples of modern rhetorical investigations that relate to interests underlying
this study can be found in Patton (1979) and Goodwin and Wenzel (1979).

/8/   Twenty-three pairs of Plutarch's *Lives* are extant. Paired composition hardly began with Plutarch; Cornelius Nepos had composed a series of short *Lives* of outstanding generals, and, in fact, comparison of generals or statesmen was common enough in the schools of Greece. It was Plutarch, though, with the encouragement of Roman friends, who first undertook the writing of an entire series of parallel *Lives*. In addition to the *Parallel Lives*, four separate *Lives* by Plutarch are extant–*Artaxerxes*, *Aratus*, *Galba*, and *Otho*. For discussion of these matters, see Erbse (398–424); Barrow (51–53); Wardman (3, 236–237).

/9/   The concept of aphoristic interaction is partly influenced by Aune's category of "gnomic" wisdom story, in which "the opinion of a sage is solicited and instantaneously obtained by a friendly and admiring interlocutor" (66). The concept of aphoristic interaction has also been influenced by Wheelwright (45–69) and by Tannehill (1975: 39–58; 1980a:138–150; forthcoming). In this paper, the term "primary character" is used in a broader sense than by Tannehill. For Tannehill, the primary character is always the person who makes the climactic pronouncement in the story. His definition is highly influenced, therefore, by a focus on individual units as discrete rhetorical units that could exist outside their present narrative context. In our study, the primary character is the person who is the center of attention in the narrative context. In other words, our study is designed to describe the dynamics of the story in its overall setting where that setting is essential for understanding the function of the story as a rhetorical unit. The difference reflects a shift from form analysis that presupposes a *Sitz im Leben* for the form outside its present literary context and form analysis concerned with the structural and linguistic dimensions of the form in its present literary setting (cf. Güttgemanns: 321–333).
      In most of the pronouncement stories analyzed in this paper, the primary character is the person who makes the final pronouncement. In two kinds of stories, the rebuff and the laudation, a named or unnamed person ends the story with a climactic saying to or about the subject of the *Life*. In these instances, the rhetorical function of the story concerns the protagonist in the overall narrative, i.e., the subject of the *Life*. In the rebuff and the laudation stories, therefore, we will refer to the subject of the *Life* as the primary character and the person who makes the climactic pronouncement as a secondary character.

/10/   Simply because a saying and a situation should be integrated by means of a pronouncement story does not mean they always are. Sayings are often attractive enough apart from the setting with which they are associated that they are transmitted in isolation from the setting or applied to another situation.

/11/   Aune (65) discusses this part of Gemoll's work and cites ἐρωτηθείς . . . ἀποκρίναιο as a verbal alternative. Gotoff (1981) also cites this aspect of Gemoll's work. Our analysis suggests that ἔφη is another common variant in the final part of the unit, while the first part may contain a genitive absolute construction containing πυνθανομένου.

/12/   Those with the classic structure: *Cicero* XXIV.6 (3); XXV.5 (4); *Demosthenes* X.2 (1); XI.4; *Alexander* IX.12–14 (6); XV.9 (5); LX.14 (8). Some which approximate the classic structure: *Alexander* IV.10 (5); XIV.4 (2); XXII.1; XXXII.2–3 (1–2).

/13/   The term "adversative" pronouncement story is partly influenced by Aune's category of "agonistic" wisdom story, in which "the sage is (unsuccessfully) challenged by a difficult question, problem, or situation for the specific purpose of testing his reported sagacity" (66). It was necessary, however, to broaden the category to account for the various kinds of struggle, contest, and challenge that exist in Plutarch's stories. In this study, the term "adversative" refers to tensive interaction which is characterized by alteration, reversal, or negation.

/14/   Both Aune and Tannehill appear to presuppose only direct confrontation (second person interaction) in wisdom or pronouncement stories. At the present time, it appears to me that differentiation between first, second, and third person interaction may yield some important conclusions about the differences between various bodies of literature in late antiquity.

/15/   See Poulos: ##1, 4, 6, where the inquiries, corrections, and descriptions total 76.5 percent of the pronouncement stories in Diogenes Laertius' *Lives*.

/16/   See Tannehill, forthcoming: n. 12, where Tannehill says that the correction "is the most common type of apophthegm in Diogenes Laertius' *Lives and Opinions of Eminent Philosophers*, Lucian's *Demonax*, Philostratus' *Life of Apollonius of Tyana*, and (pseudo?)-Plutarch's *Sayings of Kings and Commanders*, among other works."

/17/   I am deeply grateful to the National Endowment for the Humanities for financial support of a research assistant during the middle stage of the analysis that led to this classification system. I wish also to thank the research assistant, Ann Burger, and two previous assistants, Richard DeMaris and Sarah Glenn DeMaris, who aided this research.

WORKS CONSULTED

Albertz, Martin
1921   *Die synoptischen Streitgespräche: Ein Beitrag zur Formengeschichte des Urchristentums*. Berlin: Trowitzsch.

Aune, David E.
1978   "Septem Sapientium Convivium (Moralia 146B–164D)." Pp. 51–105 in *Plutarch's Ethical Writings and Early Christian Literature*. Ed. Hans Dieter Betz. Studia ad Corpus Hellenisticum Novi Testamenti 4. Leiden: E. J. Brill.

Barrow, Reginald H.
1967   *Plutarch and His Times*. Bloomington: Indiana University.

Betz, Hans Dieter
1978   "De Laude Ipsius (Moralia 539A–547F)." Pp. 367–393 in *Plutarch's Ethical Writings and Early Christian Literature*. Ed. Hans Dieter Betz. Studia ad Corpus Hellenisticum Novi Testamenti 4. Leiden: E. J. Brill.

Bousset, Wilhelm
1923   *Apophthegmata: Studien zur Geschichte des ältesten Mönchtums*. Ed. G. Hermann and Th. Krüger. Tübingen: J. C. B. Mohr.

Bultmann, Rudolf
1921   *Die Geschichte der synoptischen Tradition*. Göttingen: Vandenhoeck und Ruprecht.

Dibelius, Martin
1919   *Die Formgeschichte des Evangeliums.* Tübingen: J. C. B. Mohr.

Erbse, Hartmut
1957   "Die Bedeutung der Synkrisis in der Parallelbiographien Plutarchs."
               Hermes 84: 398–424.

Fascher, Erich
1924   *Die formgeschichtliche Methode.* BZNW 2. Giessen: Töpelmann.

Fiebig, Paul
1925   *Der Erzählungsstil der Evangelien.* Leipzig: Hinrichs.

Fischel, Henry A.
1968   "Studies in Cynicism and the Ancient Near East: The Transformation
               of a *Chria.*" Pp. 372–411 in *Religions in Antiquity.* Ed. Jacob
               Neusner. Studies in the History of Religions, Supplements to *Numen*
               14. Leiden: E. J. Brill.

1969   "Story and History: Observations on Greco-Roman Rhetoric and Phari-
               saism." Pp. 56–88 in *American Oriental Society, Middle Western
               Branch, Semi-Centennial Volume.* Ed. Denis Sinor. Oriental Series 3.
               Bloomington, Ind.: Asian Studies Research Institute.

1973   *Rabbinic Literature and Greco-Roman Philosophy.* Leiden: E. J. Brill.

Gemoll, Wilhelm
1924   *Das Apophthegma: Literarhistorische Studien.* Vienna and Leipzig.

Goodwin, Paul D., and Wenzel, Joseph W.
1979   "Proverbs and Practical Reasoning: A Study in Socio-Logic." *The
               Quarterly Journal of Speech* 65: 289–302.

Gotoff, Harold C.
1979   *Cicero's Elegant Style.* Urbana: University of Illinois.

1981   "Cicero's Style for Relating Memorable Sayings." *Illinois Classical
               Studies* 6.2:294–316.

Güttgemanns, Erhardt
1979   *Candid Questions concerning Gospel Form Criticism.* Trans. W. G.
               Doty. Pittsburgh Theological Monograph 26. Pittsburgh: Pickwick.

Neusner, Jacob
1970   *Development of a Legend: Studies on the Traditions concerning
               Yoḥanan ben Zakkai.* Studia Post-Biblica 16. Leiden: E. J. Brill.

1971   *The Rabbinic Traditions about the Pharisees before 70. Part III:*
                Conclusions. Leiden: E. J. Brill.

Patton, John H.
1979   "Causation and Creativity in Rhetorical Situations: Distinctions and
                Implications." *The Quarterly Journal of Speech* 65: 36-55.

Poulos, Paula Nassen
1981   "Form and Function of the Pronouncement Story in Diogenes Laer-
                tius' *Lives.*" In this volume.

Spencer, Richard A.
1977   "'Apophthegm' and Related Terms in the Works of Hellenistic Gram-
                marians and Rhetoricians." Unpublished manuscript distributed to Pro-
                nouncement Story Work Group, San Francisco.

Tannehill, Robert C.
1975   *The Sword of His Mouth.* Philadelphia and Missoula: Fortress and
                Scholars.
1980a   "Tension in Synoptic Sayings and Stories." *Interpretation* 34: 138–150.
1980b   "Attitudinal Shift in Synoptic Pronouncement Stories." Pp. 183–97 in
                Richard A. Spencer (ed.), *Orientation by Disorientation: Studies in
                Literary Criticism and Biblical Literary Criticism in Honor of
                William A. Beardslee.* Pittsburgh: Pickwick.
forthcoming   "Types and Functions of Apophthegms in the Synoptic Gospels." In
                Aufstieg und Niedergang der römischen Welt. Ed. Hildegard Tem-
                porini and Wolfgang Haase. Band II.25.1.

Wardman, Alan E.
1974   *Plutarch's Lives.* Berkeley and Los Angeles: University of California.

von Wartensleben, G.
1901   *Begriff der griechischen Chreia und Beiträge zur Geschichte ihrer
                Form.* Heidelberg: Carl Winter's Universitätsbuchhandlung.

Wheelwright, Philip
1962   *Metaphor and Reality.* Bloomington: Indiana University.

Ziegler, Kurt
1951   "Plutarchos von Chaironeia." *Paulys Real-Encyclopädie der classi-
                schen Altertumswissenschaft* 21.1: 636–962.

FORM AND FUNCTION OF THE
PRONOUNCEMENT STORY IN DIOGENES
LAERTIUS' *LIVES*

Paula Nassen Poulos

ABSTRACT

The nearly five hundred pronouncement stories in Diogenes Laertius' *Lives*
can be divided into six types: inquiries, quests, objections, corrections, commendations,
and descriptions. This essay indicates the percentage of pronouncement stories in the
Lives which belong to each type, offers examples of each type, and discusses some of
the variations within the types. Nearly all the pronouncement stories in the *Lives* can
be included in these six types.

0.1   One of the best presentations of the pronouncement story in Greek
literature is Diogenes Laertius' *Lives and Opinions of Eminent Philosophers* (third century C.E.). In this compendium of ten books describing the
lives and doctrines of eighty-two sages and philosophers who lived in the
five centuries before our common era, Diogenes Laertius has related the
works and sayings of figures from Thales to Epicurus, recording for
posterity, often in the form of a story, the perceptive observations and clever
remarks attributed to these figures as they taught in their schools, associated
with their students, and commented on the human condition.

0.2   Diogenes Laertius was prolific in his use of the pronouncement
story or apophthegm (two terms which will be used interchangeably) as he
highlighted the features of the philosophers' lives. His series of anecdotal
biographies has produced nearly five hundred (493) stories which can be
characterized as pronouncement stories. For the most part, they appear
fairly evenly distributed throughout the lives, though the heaviest concentra-
tions are in the lives of Aristippus (2.65–104), Diogenes the Cynic (6.20–81),
and Zeno (7.1–160).

0.3   Such stories have two basic components— a stimulus and response
or setting and response— which are generally striking in their interaction.

The stimulus may be verbal and/or non-verbal. The response, though usually verbal, sometimes combines both words and action; occasionally there is a significant action which substitutes for the expected words /1/. Noting the relationship which exists between a setting and response is important in reading a pronouncement story and discovering its theme and purpose.

0.4   Fundamental to my effort to establish a typology depicting these relationships in Diogenes Laertius' *Lives* has been the work of Professor Robert C. Tannehill. In his attempt to afford classification to almost every type of pronouncement story, from the simplest topic/comment to the most elaborately developed narrative/response, he has moved, in recent articles, toward establishing a clear, concise typology for apophthegms. This typology includes: inquiries, quests, objections, corrections, commendations, and descriptions (see Tannehill, 1980, forthcoming, and the introductory essay in the present volume).

Using these categories as the basis for examining the pronouncement stories in the *Lives*, I have been interested to note that, for the most part, these stories have fit rather easily into the six types; not only have these classifications appeared appropriate for the study of New Testament stories, but for a close reading of Diogenes Laertius' philosophical text as well. Nevertheless, inevitable differences have been observed in the form and function of Diogenes' stories, and these are discussed in the following pages.

0.5   There is great variety in the pronouncement stories that are represented in the typology. There are the short and the long, the serious and the witty, the prosaic and the clever, the profound and the superficial. There are those in which the key figure answers questions or requests (e.g., inquiries or quests) and those in which he reacts to people's assumptions or positions, or comments on situations which he has observed (e.g., objections, corrections, commendations, descriptions). Yet, for all the variations, it is the striking combination of stimulus and response which accounts for the genre's unity. The typology:

1.   *Inquiries.* These are the pronouncement stories that begin with an open question or request for advice or information. In the *Lives*, eighteen percent of the stories fall into this classification, one-third of which appear in Book 1 dealing with the sages. Not surprisingly it was the sages and philosophers who were sought out for their wise answers. The form of the inquiries is basically simple; the stimulus is verbal in each instance, as is expected, and the responses are verbal too, though there are several occasions when an act reinforces the saying. A few of the stories also contain elements of humor in the answer.

1.1   For the most part, these apophthegms begin with a nonchallenging question. The question is considered legitimate by the sage, and he answers it. Examples /2/:

To the question, "What among men is both good and bad?" his [Anacharsis'] answer was "The tongue." (1.105)

Being asked wherein lies the difference between the educated and the uneducated, Chilon answered, "In good hope." What is hard? "To keep a secret, to employ leisure well, to be able to bear an injury." (1.69)

When a lad from Pontus was about to attend his lectures, and asked him what he required, the [Antisthenes'] answer was, "Come with a new book, a new pen, and new tablets, if you have a mind to." (6.3)

To the question what wine he found pleasant to drink, he [Diogenes] replied, "That for which other people pay." (6.54)

The various types of questions put to the sages are evident in these examples. They range from the serious to the commonplace to the nonsensical. In the third example there is even a skillful play on words (if the Greek word *kainou* is read as a single word, it means "new," but if it is read as two words, it means "and a mind"), so the phrase "a new book" might also be translated as "a book and a mind," with the same interpretation possible for reading the phrases "a new pen, and new tablets." Most often the setting is simple, consisting solely of a question (examples 1 and 2), but sometimes the question is part of a more complete descriptive setting. Since the majority of these stories is of the brief question/answer type where the contribution of the setting is minimal and the identity of the questioner unknown, the forcefulness of the story depends almost solely on the effectiveness of the response itself. The sage is given ample opportunity to be wise and/or clever.

Because any story beginning with a neutral question or request is placed in this category, it is, of necessity, general in nature. This feature provides it with its flexibility but also with a certain awkwardness. Since the range of questions and answers is very broad, there is no common theme to aid in the further analysis of the passages.

1.2   There is a subtype of inquiries, however, that does have a central theme. It is the group of questlike inquiries which also begin with an open question. In the *Lives*, six such stories have been identified in which verbal responses are made to the question. As the questioner confronts the philosopher in these apophthegms, he seeks to discover what is best in life, how to live well, and how to find happiness. Examples:

To the question how shall we lead the best and most righteous life, Thales' answer was, "By refraining from doing what we blame in others." (1.36)

To the question what man is happy, Thales' answer was, "He who has a healthy body, a resourceful mind and a docile nature." (1.37)

Being asked what was the height of human bliss, he [Antisthenes] replied, "To die happy." (6.5)

> Someone asked him [Antisthenes] what he must do to be good and noble, and he replied, "You must learn from those who know that the faults you have are to be avoided." (6.8)

Although these questlike stories are simple in structure, consisting of only the question and answer, they represent serious concerns in people's lives; they concentrate on worthwhile earthly pursuits and ways to live life to the fullest. These are not true quests, however (see the discussion of quests below), because the story does not go beyond a single verbal exchange. The hearer/reader does not have the opportunity to participate emotionally in the quester's search or to learn of the success or failure of the quest.

1.3   Another subtype of inquiry is the testing inquiry. This classification includes any story which begins with a special question or request designed to test the philosopher or to discover how wise or clever he is. The *Lives* surprisingly yield only one such pronouncement story:

> Being asked what kind of hound (*kyōn*) he was, he [Diogenes] replied, "When hungry, a Maltese; when full, a Molossian—two breeds which most people praise, though for fear of fatigue they do not venture out hunting with them. So neither can you live with me, because you are afraid of the discomforts." (6.55)

Here we have a good example of a skillful sage giving an impressive answer when put to the test. Diogenes the Cynic (doglike) turns a derogatory question into a personal compliment of his own uniqueness and worth as an individual and thinker in society (in the Greek world of fourth century B.C.E. Since open hostility is apparent on the part of the questioner here, there is the tension which characterizes a testing question.

It seems unusual to note that, of all the stories beginning with a question in the eighty-two lives of the sages, this is the only testing inquiry. More apophthegms showing the wisdom of the philosophers being challenged and tested by detractors and followers alike are expected (cf. Jesus in the *Gospels*). Instead, Diogenes Laertius uses the question to introduce general inquiries, as well as a large number of objections, corrections, and descriptions.

2.   *Quests*. There are several characteristics of a true quest story: a person making a request or seeking something of personal importance from a philosopher or sage, a certain tension in the story, felt by the reader/hearer, as to whether the quest will end in success or failure, especially if obstacles appear in the path leading to the goal, and a final indication of success or failure. Diogenes Laertius relates the following quest story, together with an alternate version by Diocles; these are the only examples found in the *Lives* (as with the testing inquiries, the reasons for the rarity of this type are unclear).

Someone wanted to study philosophy under him. Diogenes gave him a tuna to carry and told him to follow him. And when for shame the man threw it away and departed, some time later on meeting him, he [Diogenes] laughed and said, "The friendship between you and me was broken by a tuna." (6.36)

When someone said to him, "Lay your commands upon us, Diogenes," he took him away and gave him a cheese to carry which cost half an obol. When the other declined, he remarked, "The friendship between you and me is broken by a little cheese worth half an obol." (6.36)

These pronouncement stories are longer and more developed than about eighty-five percent of the apophthegms in the *Lives*; there is a series of exchanges between the parties. In each case, someone approaches Diogenes the philosopher, seeks to become a student or to learn from him, and then fails to attain the goal of his quest because the cost of discipleship is too high. Diogenes' final remark emphasizes the disparity between the hope and the reality.

Unlike the one example of a failed quest in the synoptics (Mark 10:17-22 par.), in which the rich man is asked to sell all that he has and give to the poor before he can follow Jesus and inherit eternal life, the sacrifice demanded of these questers by Diogenes seems of very small consequence. Yet, as Diogenes demonstrated, if they truly wished to learn from him the precepts of the Cynics, a philosophical school which stressed that virtue and happiness consist in self-control and independence, it was necessary for them to overcome the obstacle of shame and embarrassment before they could become his followers. It is interesting to note that, even though the identity of the questers is unknown, these stories have a certain emotional appeal for the reader; from the time of the request to the moment of failure, there is involvement with, if not sympathy for, the seeker.

3.   *Objections.* In these stories one or more people find fault with the behavior or speech of a philosopher and reproach him for it. Sometimes the objection is made in the form of a question as to the reason for such behavior. Since justification for his words or deeds is implicitly or explicitly requested in the objection, a sense of conflict and tension is evident before the sage makes his reply. However, the tension is always resolved when the sage vindicates himself, often eloquently and cleverly.

Almost twenty percent of the pronouncement stories in the *Lives* are classified here. Examples:

Being once reproached for giving alms to a bad man, he [Aristotle] rejoined, "It was the man and not his character that I pitied." (5.17)

When he was reproached for not paying court to a youth, his [Bion's] excuse was, "You can't get hold of a soft cheese with a hook." (4.47)

To one who accused him of living with a courtesan, he [Aristippus] put the question, "Why, is there any difference between taking a house in which many people have lived before and taking one in which nobody has ever lived?" The answer being "No," he continued, "Or again, between sailing in a ship in which 10,000 people have sailed before and in one in which nobody has ever sailed?" "There is no difference." "Then it makes no difference," said he, "whether the woman you live with has lived with many or with nobody." (2.74)

He [Heraclitus] would retire to the temple of Artemis and play at knuckle-bones with the boys; and when the Ephesians stood around him and looked on, "Why, you rascals," he said, "are you astonished? Is it not better to do this than to take part in your civil life?" (9.3)

It happened once that he set sail for Corinth and, being overtaken by a storm, he [Aristippus] was in great consternation. Someone said, "We plain men are not alarmed, and are you philosophers turned cowards?" To this he replied, "The lives at stake in the two cases are not comparable." (2.71)

When someone inquired, "Have you no concern in your native land?" "Gently," he [Anaxagoras] replied, "I am greatly concerned with my fatherland," and pointed to the sky. (2.7)

These examples illustrate the several different forms that the objection stories take. The first two passages are typical of the majority of this class, which consists of a brief stimulus and response that are both verbal. In the third example, the usual briefly stated objection is followed by an extended verbal dialogue between the parties. The fourth represents the few stories that feature a non-verbal stimulus but a spoken response; the fifth, those stories with a more elaborately depicted setting; and the sixth, while introduced by the familiar short question, concludes with a saying and act combined.

3.1   Sometimes an apophthegm may contain a special feature. In the following examples note the humor in the first story and the perfect balance of phrases in the second:

He [Aristippus] made a request to Dionysius on behalf of a friend, and failing to obtain it, fell down at his feet. When someone jeered at him, he made the reply, "It is not I who am to blame but Dionysius who has ears in his feet." (2.79)

When some Athenian reproached him with being a Scythian, he [Anacharsis] replied, "Well, granted that my country is a disgrace to me, but you are a disgrace to your country." (1.104)

3.2   The objection stories, because of the distinctiveness of their style, presented no problems in terms of classification. The setting, in virtually every story, is characterized either by a Greek word expressing reproach or censure on the part of the objector or by a markedly accusatory or condescending tone. Diogenes Laertius sometimes reveals the name of the objector, particularly in those stories displaying the rivalry which existed between the philosophical schools, but, for the most part, the characters remain anonymous. The central moment, however, belongs to the sage when he meets the challenge to defend himself by tersely, but cleverly, attributing the reproach to the objector's lack of insight or wisdom or narrowness of vision regarding the important things in life.

4.   *Corrections.* These are the stories in which a sense of conflict is created by a philosopher when he makes a corrective judgment regarding a person or scene which he has just encountered. In his response to a particular setting, he may correct an assumption that he considers erroneous behind a request, question, stat action; or the correction may simply follow the description of some situation.

This classification, consisting of fifty-one percent of the stories, is the largest one of the typology and, together with the objections, comprises seventy percent of all of the pronouncement stories in the *Lives.* Since the tone of these apophthegms is so distinctive, there was little difficulty in establishing this category. Examples:

When a friend complained to him that he had lost his notes, "You should have inscribed them," said he [Antisthenes], "on your mind instead of on paper." (6.5)

To one who said "You have been deprived of the Athenians," he [Anaxagoras] said, "No, but they have been deprived of me." (2.10)

Plato had defined Man as an animal, biped and featherless, and was applauded. Diogenes plucked a fowl and brought it into the lecture room with the words, "Here is Plato's man." (6.40)

On coming to Myndus and finding the gates large, though the city itself was very small, he [Diogenes] cried, "Men of Myndus, bar your gates, lest the city run away." (6.57)

One day as he entered the house of a courtesan, one of the lads with him blushed, whereupon he [Aristippus] remarked, "It is not going in that is dangerous, but being unable to go out." (2.69)

When a stupid fellow related something to him with no apparent object, he [Menedemus] inquired if he had a farm. And hearing that he had and that there was a large stock of cattle on it, he said, "Then go and look after them, lest it should happen that they are ruined and a clever farmer thrown away." (2.128)

Not being able to curb the extravagance of someone who had invited him to dinner, he [Menedemus] said nothing when he was invited, but rebuked his host tacitly by confining himself to olives. (2.129)

As observed in the objection stories, there is variety of form in these corrective pronouncements, too. The settings of approximately two-thirds of the apophthegms are verbal. All but a dozen responses are verbal and appear to be fairly evenly divided between responses that are volunteered by the sage and those that are requested in some manner. The examples above are representative of the various types of combinations: a verbal stimulus in indirect discourse and a verbal response in direct discourse (#1); a verbal stimulus in direct discourse and a verbal response in direct discourse (#2); a verbal stimulus and combined verbal/non-verbal response (#3); a non-verbal (a scene, an action) stimulus and verbal response (#4,5); a verbal stimulus and verbal response in the form of a dialogue (#6); a non-verbal stimulus and a non-verbal response (#7).

This variety in form lends interest to these pronouncement stories as they run the gamut from forthright correction to gentle dissuasion, from seriousness to playful humor. In story after story, the sages make the perceptively wise, corrective judgments that realign displaced values and reassert the quality of life, break illusions which have been wrongly created, and play upon the absurdities of commonplace situations.

5.   *Commendations.* This type, the complement of corrections, is marked by a philosopher's responding affirmatively to a person or position described in the setting. In the response which he makes, he gives praise and commendation to something which a person has said or done or advocated, often revealing a previously hidden value or importance in the person or quality which he is affirming.

In the *Lives*, only two percent of the stories have been identified as commendations. With regard to form, where the stimulus is verbal, the expected answer is given verbally; where the setting is non-verbal, the response appears to be spoken voluntarily by the sage. Examples:

One day he [Diogenes] detected a youth blushing. "Be of courage," he said, "that is the hue of virtue." (6.54)

One day observing a youth studying philosophy, he [Diogenes] said, "Well done, Philosophy, because you divert admirers of bodily charms to the real beauty of the soul." (6.58)

His opinion of himself was so high that when someone inquired, "To whom shall I entrust my son?" he [Chrysippus] replied, "To me; for if I had dreamt of there being anyone better than myself, I should be studying with him myself." (7.183)

5.1   Sometimes it is necessary for the philosopher to correct a misconception or false assumption before the true value of what he is commending can be seen. The following examples combine the elements of correction and commendation:

Aeschines said to him, "I am a poor man and have nothing else to give, but I offer you myself," and Socrates answered, "Nay, don't you see that you are offering me the greatest gift of all?" (2.34)

> On being asked by a tyrant what bronze is best for a statue, he [Diogenes] replied, "That of which Harmodius and Aristogeiton were moulded." (6.50)

It should be noted that it was Harmodius and Aristogeiton who were famous for their attempt to kill the Athenian tyrant, Hippias, and his brother, Hipparchus, at the festival of the Panathenaea in 514 B.C.E.

5.2   There is also an example in the *Lives* of a hybrid objection-commendation story:

> There was a stout musician whom everybody depreciated and Diogenes alone praised. When asked why, he said, "Because being so big, he yet sings to his lute and does not turn brigand." (6.47)

5.3   These commendations, whether in pure or hybrid form, underscore for the reader/hearer the qualities and values in life which the philosophers consider worthy of emulation. In these stories not only are the sages representative of these values but the commended figures as well. Whether praising a virtuous youth or the devoted study of philosophy, opposition to tyranny or frugality of living, these stories stress positive values and the people who embace them, correcting and objecting to the competing values upheld by society.

6.   *Descriptions*. Pronouncement stories in which the philosopher's primary interest is in describing a situation, scene, action, or person in a fitting or striking way are assigned to this category. The evaluation process, so characteristic of corrections and commendations, does not play a part. The sage rather focuses on the poignant or incongruous qualities of a setting in making his response.

Descriptions comprise about seven and one-half percent of the stories which appear in the *Lives*. In these apophthegms the setting is verbal almost as often as it is non-verbal, while all responses are verbal, though occasionally accompanied by an act. Whereas two-thirds of the responses are volunteered by the sage (particularly when the setting is non-verbal), the rest are given upon request. Examples:

> When mice crept onto the table, he [Diogenes] addressed them thus, "See, now even Diogenes keeps parasites." (6.40)

> When news was brought him that he was condemned and his sons were dead, his [Anaxagoras'] comment on the sentence was, "Long ago nature condemned both my judges and me to death"; and on his sons, "I knew that my children were born to die." (2.13)

> To a slanderer who showed a grave face, he [Bion] said, "I don't know whether you have met with ill luck or your neighbor with good." (4.51)

When a little sparrow was pursued by a hawk and rushed into his bosom, he [Xenocrates] stroked it and let it go, declaring that a suppliant must not be betrayed. (4.10)

After ascertaining that the ship's side was four fingers' breadth in thickness, he [Anacharsis] remarked that the passengers were just so far from death. (1.103)

These description stories have an engaging quality about them which attracts the reader's/hearer's attention to a new way of perceiving a situation which, under ordinary circumstances, might go unnoticed or be viewed in a more predictable or traditional light. In these scenes, the sages are shown to be skillfully clever in capturing, in an epitomizing statement, the very essence of a particular scene. In humorous observations and dramatic remarks, in expressions of tenderness and sympathetic comments, they bring their special insights to the interpretation of events.

7.   With these six categories (inquiries, quests, objections, corrections, commendations, and descriptions), a basic framework is proposed for virtually every one of the nearly five hundred pronouncement stories appearing in the *Lives*. This typology is the result of a close study of philosophers' relationships with their audiences and surroundings. Although it is similar in form to the synoptic types which portray Jesus involved in like relationships (for wise men from culture to culture appear to be similarly wise in word and deed), yet, because the philosophers are wise men and not saviors, within the basic framework there are the differences in style, message, and impact of individual stories noted in the various discussions above.

7.1   The pronouncement story for Diogenes Laertius has proved to be a most effective way of presenting the doctrines and sayings of the eminent philosophers of the Greek world. In these stories, Diogenes not only describes the education and personal character of the sages but has them speak for themselves through their own clever pronouncements.

They, naturally, speak from a philosophical vantage point. As formulators of ideas, teachers of students, and sometime participants in friendly competition with members of rival schools of thought, they address the human situation; with both seriousness and humor, they reflect upon the many different aspects of their Greek culture.

As some of the quoted examples show, their message to their readers/hearers is not always profound. Yet, their pronouncements, for the most part, do seem to emphasize larger ethical concerns. The sages seek not so much to offer a vision of final and eternal things as to strip away pretence in favor of naturalness and to point the way to individual happiness; they speak of the way to live a full life, that is, how to behave and what to say in order to live a temperate and virtuous life. For the philosophers of the Hellenistic Age, speaking to people in a time of profound change and constant uncertainty, the need to address this concern for personal peace and security was especially important.

7.2   Finally, it is interesting to observe the skillful way in which Diogenes Laertius often calls attention to these pronouncements, whatever the message; in his imaginative telling of the stories, he regularly places a minimum of emphasis on a story's setting and stresses its response instead. In each of the books throughout the *Lives*, stories can be seen which illustrate this well: apophthegms in which the narrative setting is very brief (perhaps as little as one line) and apophthegms in which the secondary character confronting the philosopher is anonymous, typically drawn, or relegated to the passive voice. It is apparent that the main function of such settings for Diogenes is to highlight the wise man's response by providing the sage with a clear opportunity to demonstrate his cleverness, perceptions, and wit.

NOTES

/1/   These three possibilities correspond to three types of *chreiai* recognized by ancient scholars. See Lausberg (537–539).

/2/   In the quoted texts I generally follow the translation of R. D. Hicks in the Loeb Classical Library, but I have modified his translation in details.

WORKS CONSULTED

Diogenes Laertius
    1972   *Lives and Opinions of Eminent Philosophers.* Translated by R. D. Hicks. 2 vols. Loeb Classical Library. Cambridge: Harvard University.

Lausberg, Heinrich
    1973   *Handbuch der literarischen Rhetorik.* 2 Aufl. München: Hueber.

Tannehill, Robert C.
    1980   "Attitudinal Shift in Synoptic Pronouncement Stories." Pp. 183–197 in Richard A. Spencer (ed.), *Orientation by Disorientation: Studies in Literary Criticism and Biblical Literary Criticism in Honor of William A. Beardslee.* Pittsburgh: Pickwick.

    forthcoming   "Types and Functions of Apophthegms in the Synoptic Gospels." In *Aufstieg und Niedergang der römischen Welt*, ed. Hildegard Temporini and Wolfgang Haase, Band II.25.1.

INTERTESTAMENTAL PRONOUNCEMENT STORIES

James C. VanderKam

North Carolina State University

ABSTRACT

A survey of Jewish intertestamental literature has uncovered only 19 units that can be labeled pronouncement stories. The large majority of these come from the Testament of Job (7) and the Story of Ahiqar (10). Neither of these works appears to be Palestinian in provenance, and the Story of Ahiqar may not even be Jewish in origin.

0. Introduction

The extant documents suggest that Jewish writers of the so-called intertestamental period rarely employed the literary type "pronouncement story" that is familiar from Greek literature. It seems strange that this should be the case because the sizable intertestamental corpus includes a number of works that attempt to highlight the piety and fame of great men and women (e.g., Additions to Daniel, Joseph and Asenath, Judith, Story of Ahiqar, Testament of Job), the sorts of compositions in which one might expect to find pronouncement stories. Nevertheless, such units are seldom found, and the two books in which several appear (Story of Ahiqar and Testament of Job) are probably not Palestinian in provenance. Furthermore, the Story of Ahiqar originally may not have been a Jewish work /1/.

1. The Sources

The relatively few pronouncement stories that are classified below were collected from a survey of the following books: Additions to Esther, Assumption of Moses, 1–3 Baruch, Bel and the Dragon, Biblical Antiquities of Pseudo-Philo, Books of Adam and Eve, Ecclesiasticus, 1–2 Enoch, Epistle of Jeremiah, 1–2 Esdras, Fragments of Eupolemus (and pseudo-Eupolemus), Joseph and Asenath, Jubilees, Judith, Letter of Aristeas, Lives of the Prophets, 1–4 Maccabees, Martyrdom of Isaiah, Paraleipomena Jeremiou, Prayer of Azariah and Song of the Three Young Men, Prayer of Manasseh, Psalms

Psalms of Solomon, the Qumran literature, Sibylline Oracles III–V, Story of Ahiqar, Susanna, Testament of Abraham, Testament of Job, Testaments of the Twelve Patriarchs, Tobit, and Wisdom of Solomon.

2.   Classification

The 19 pronouncement stories which were found in this substantial body of literature can be classified in these categories:

Corrections (6): Lives of the Prophets: Daniel 17–18; Testament of
        Job 11:1–11; 12:1–6; 20:4–10; 21:1–4; 38:9–13.
Commendations (2): Testament of Job 19:1–4; 28:6–7.
Quests (0)
Objections (1): Bel and the Dragon 23–27.
Descriptions (0)
Inquiries (10): Story of Ahiqar 2:105; 6:10; 6:11; 6:12; 6:13;
        6:20–7:4; 7:5–8; 7:9–15a; 7:17–19; 7:20–21 /2/.

3.   Analysis

3.1   Corrections

3.11   Lives of the Prophets: Daniel 17–18: "The king named the prophet Baltasar because he wished to make him a joint heir with his children; but the holy man said: 'Far be it from me to forsake the heritage of my fathers and join in the inheritances of the uncircumcised'" /3/. In this passage Nebuchadnezzar makes the natural assumption that becoming a royal heir would be the coveted prize for an exile, but Daniel corrects his presupposition by appealing to a far different set of values in which his Judean heritage, though it was that of a captive people, is paradoxically appraised more highly than that of the conqueror.

3.12   Testament of Job 11:1–11: As Job related to his second family several stories that illustrated his former wealth, he told in 11:1–11 of lending money to others who, as he did, wished to help the poor but lacked his phenomenal resources. Some of those who received money from him under these circumstances were robbed of it. They desired to repay, but, after reading their note of security, Job cancelled it by declaring: "As long as I trusted you in the interests of the poor, I will take nothing from you" (11:10b). Though the narrative is somewhat extended and includes several scenes with dialogue, this declaration, which in itself is an act, is its climax and serves to correct the debtors' assumption, based on normal monetary policy, by advocating a system of values in which virtue is judged to be of greater worth than money.

3.13   Testament of Job 12:1–6: This story shares the setting of the previous one and differs only in that Job here insists on paying those who had served as volunteers at the tables where he fed the indigent. While the pronouncement in 11:10b, by its nature as a legal declaration, technically was also an act, the pronouncement in 12:5b is accompanied by a deed, viz., paying the volunteers /4/.

3.14   Testament of Job 20:4-10: An unusual correction appears at the point where the Satan has gained divine permission to deal with Job's body as he wished (20:1-3). Here Job describes one of his numerous afflictions thus: "And discharges from my body also combined to drench the ground with their moisture. There were many worms in it and if a worm fell off, I would pick it up and return it to the same place saying: 'Stay in the same place in which you were put until you receive instructions from the one who commanded you'" (20:10). Job's bizarre remonstrance and act correct the worm for its understandable capitulation to the law of gravity and commend action other than the expected. It should be noted that Job does not correct the Satan, who is his tormentor, but rather a third party, which is exhorted to obey the Satan.

3.15   Testament of Job 21:1-4: In the present story Job continues to catalogue for his children the astonishing sufferings that he had endured. In this case he recalls that, as he sat atop a dung-hill for 48 years and experienced a variety of diseases, he had the misfortune of seeing his once-prominent wife Sitidos reduced to servitude for a "certain crude person" (21:1b) in order to obtain bread for Job. In commenting on this scene, Job corrects the view of those rulers of the city who, under these changed circumstances, regarded themselves as masters and his wife as a slave: "O the pretension of the rulers of this city whom I consider unworthy even of my roving dogs. For how can they use my wife as a slave?" (21:2b-3) He seems to be asserting that the quality of the person is not reduced by loss of position nor is it increased by greater wealth.

3.16   Testament of Job 38:9-13: This pericope, which is part of a larger scene in which the three kings and Job are debating his condition, is set off from the preceding section (36:1-38:8) by a change of speaker from Baldas (biblical Bildad) to Sophar and by a change of subject from Job's mental to his physical condition. Sophar offers to Job use of the kings' physicians, but, as he frequently does in this book, the devastated patriarch moves beyond earthly phenomena to heavenly realities. He corrects his comforters' assumption that doctors could aid him, confessing: "My healing and treatment are from the Lord, who created even the physicians" (38:13b) /5/.

3.2   Commendations

3.21   Testament of Job 19:1-4: The Satan's efforts to unravel Job's piety eventually reached the extreme of killing his ten children. The present unit depicts Job's initial puzzled response to the arrival of the messenger who carried the crushing news (v 1). But the story reaches its culmination at that moment when Job, after reflection, perceives the deeper meaning and purpose beneath the surface events. He then commends the deity with the familiar words: "The Lord has given, the Lord has taken away. As the Lord decided, so has it happened. Blessed be the name of the Lord." An element of paradox in the commendation is unmistakable.

3.22   Testament of Job 28:6–7: Chap. 28 describes the arrival of the three kings and their astonishment at the condition of Job, whom they had known as an extremely wealthy man. Job, who continues to be the narrator, inserts within this context a short reference to previous occasions when the kings had come and had marvelled at his possessions. Then they had commended him thus: "Whenever the goods of us three kings are brought together at the same place, they by no means match the glorious stones of your kingdom. For you are more noble (*eugenesteros*) than those from the east" (28:6b–7). While the word *eugenesteros* can carry the meaning *generous*, the context suggests that the kings are here using wealth as a measure of nobility /6/.

3.3   Objections

      Bel and the Dragon 23–27: The stimulus for the scene is the king's objection to what he correctly assumed would be Daniel's attitude regarding the divinity of the dragon whom the Babylonians worshiped. After describing Daniel's actions (he fed the beast a disagreeable cake of fat, pitch, and hair which caused it to explode), the story reaches its climax in his triumphant question to the king: "Weren't you worshiping this, Your Majesty?" /7/ Daniel's rhetorical question does provide a striking conclusion for the story, but it certainly shares the spotlight with his action.

3.4   Inquiries

3.41   Story of Ahiqar 2:105 (Armenian only): "They asked the sage and said: What is the most pleasing thing on earth? He replied: Modesty. He that hath a modest face is pleasing. For all evils are born of impudence and folly." Since both the Syriac and Arabic versions lack this passage, it is textually highly suspect. As it stands, it is a pronouncement story in which the simplest of narratives sets the stage for Ahiqar's sage reply. There is no hint of hostility between the questioners and Ahiqar; they simply wish to elicit information from this fountain of wisdom.

3.42   The remaining nine pronouncement stories in the Story of Ahiqar are also inquiries and can be divided into two groups: those that culminate in a saying and those that are dominated by a saying and an action. As all members of each group exhibit the same formal structure, study of a single example from each group will suffice. All nine stories appear within the broader context of a contest between the monarchs of Egypt and Assyria, with Ahiqar, as the unrecognized representative of Sennacherib, being challenged by the pharaoh and his court in a variety of circumstances /8/.

3.421   In 6:10 (Syriac; Armenian; Arabic 6:14b–16) the following scene is described:

> Then the king commanded his nobles, "On the morrow clothe yourselves in red," and the king dressed himself in fine linen, and sat on his throne. And he commanded and I came into his presence: and he said to me, "To what am I like, Abikam [=Ahiqar], and to what are my nobles like?" And I answered and said to him, "My lord the king, thou art like unto Bel, and thy nobles are like unto his priests." And again he said to me, "Go to thy lodging, and come to me on the morrow."

The only issue here is whether the wise man can respond in a convincingly flattering and witty way to the scene which is staged before him. In other words, there is a testing quality to the pharaoh's inquiry; the questions are meant to trap Ahiqar, though, of course, he deftly sidesteps the trap. The remaining three stories in this category (6:11 [Syriac; Armenian 6:11–12; Arabic 6:17–18; Greek 28]; 6:12 [Syriac; Arabic 6:19–20; lacking in Armenian and Greek]; and 6:13 [Syriac; Armenian 6:13–14; Arabic 6:21–22; cf. Greek 28]) differ from 6:10 only in the colors of the clothing in which the court is dressed and in the vocabulary of Ahiqar's replies.

3.422   In 6:20–7:4 (Syriac; Armenian 6:25–7.5; Arabic 6:30–7:4; Greek 32) the pharaoh orders Ahiqar to tell him "a word which I never heard nor any one of my nobles, and which was never heard in the city of my kingdom" (6:20b Syriac). Ahiqar then composed a letter which purported to come from the pharaoh and to be addressed to Sennacherib. In it the Egyptian monarch requested a loan of 900 silver talents and promised to repay (7:1–2 Syriac). When he read the forged letter before the court, they responded, as they had been instructed, that they had heard this before. Ahiqar then observed: "Behold, [in that case] there is a debt of 900 talents from Egypt to Assyria" (7:4b Syriac). There is again a testing atmosphere here, but the hero handles his exacting assignment with a wondrous flair. While his reponse includes both an action (writing and reading the letter) and a statement, in this instance the pronouncement appears to be the dominant element (cf. also 7:9–15a [Syriac; Armenian 6:22–24; Arabic 7:9–15a; Greek 30]). In other stories from this group, however, deeds assume a greater prominence vis-à-vis statements. For example, when the pharaoh challenges him to build a castle in the air (7:5–8 [Syriac; Armenian 6:7–8 lacks the pronouncement; Arabic 7:5–8; Greek 28–29]) or to fashion a rope from sand (7:17–19 [Syriac; Armenian 6:25a, 7:4–5a; Arabic 7:15b–16]), Ahiqar's execution of these tasks is at least as prominent as the witty sayings that conclude the tales.

4.   Conclusion

There are other passages within intertestamental literature that share some of the traits of pronouncement stories (e.g., the 72 questions and answers in the Letter of Aristeas 187–294), but these belong, in the final analysis, to other literary categories. Thus a search for intertestamental pronouncement stories has produced relatively meagre results for so large a body of literature, but this rather negative conclusion has some value in that it strongly suggests that the authors of the synoptic pronouncement stories drew their inspiration for them from other quarters.

NOTES

/1/   The Story of Ahiqar originated no later than the fifth century B.C., the date of a fragmentary Aramaic text of the book found at Elephantine (for introduction, text, translation, and notes, see Cowley: 204–248). The story itself is probably still older and may have been composed in a Mesopotamian environment (Cowley: 205–208). It falls, therefore, outside the normal limits for intertestamental literature, but it is usually included among the pseudepigrapha perhaps because it is a non-biblical work that seems to have been popular among Jews of this period (cf. Tob 1:21–22; 2:10; 11:16–19; 14:10). Citations of the Story of Ahiqar are taken from Conybeare, Harris, and Lewis, 1913; the texts of non-Aramaic versions can be consulted in Conybeare, Harris, and Lewis, 1898.

The Testament of Job can tentatively be assigned a date in the first century A.D. (cf. Denis: 103). Philonenko (41–53) has adduced evidence which suggests a link between it and the Egyptian Therapeutae whom Philo described. He also believes that it was composed in Greek. Quotations of the Testament of Job are from Kraft's translation.

/2/   None of the passages considered in this essay has been preserved in the Aramaic fragments of the Story of Ahiqar; consequently, one must resort to the later versions. The references given here are for the Syriac version, but, since verse numbering differs from version to version, the locations in the other versions will be given for each passage that is discussed.

/3/   The quotation is taken from Torrey's translation. He and others have dated the Lives of the Prophets to the first century A.D. (Torrey: 11–12; cf. Denis: 89–90). Though there is dispute about its original language, the earliest extant version is the Greek one. The text certainly appears to be Jewish, but it does have some Christian interpolations (see the Jeremiah section).

/4/   It should be noted that in 11:1–11 and 12:1–6 the saying does not assume the importance in the story that one normally finds in the synoptic pronouncement stories. They are verbal complements of Job's charitable acts in each case, and it is the acts that are the most significant element in the stories.

/5/   It is possible that Testament of Job 13:1–6 should also be classified as a correction, but it has been omitted from the list primarily because of what seems to be a textual problem. The statement of Job's servants that would presumably be the pronouncement ("Who will provide for us from his meats that we might be filled?" v 5b) makes little sense in connection with the following line: "Yet I [Job] was exceedingly kind!" (v 6; the word *yet* reflects nothing in the

Greek text). This line should be a continuation of v 5b, but as it now reads it contradicts it (cf. Kraft's conjecture in the note to 13:5b). If a better text becomes available and this passage proves to be a correction, it would be an inverted one, since Job's servants would be correcting him for neglecting their needs in his zeal to aid the poor.

Testament of Job 36:1–38:8 also exhibits some characteristics of a correction, though its length and the variety of elements in the story indicate that it is not a single pronouncement story. The element of correction arises in the context in which Baldas questions Job about his mental stability. His queries seem to assume an earthbound understanding of stability, and this Job corrects in the concluding pronouncement: "If you do not understand the functions of the body, how will you understand the heavenly matters?" (38:8; cf. Mark 11:27–33)

/6/   Testament of Job 41:1–42:8 should also be mentioned in this context. While its complicated structure suggests that it is not a single story which is dominated by one climactic statement, it contains an element of correction for Eliphaz and his two friends (42:3b–5) and of commendation for Job (42:4, 6).

/7/   This is the translation of Moore (143) and is the reading of the LXX. The text of Theodotion has: "Look at what you were worshiping!" (Moore: 140).

/8/   The inquiries in the Story of Ahiqar clearly should be numbered among the fairly widely attested stories about wisdom contests at royal courts (for other Jewish examples, see the Letter of Aristeas 187–294 and 1 Esdr 3:1–4:42). Nevertheless, these stories about Ahiqar do meet the criteria for pronouncement stories and should therefore be included in this study.

WORKS CONSULTED

Conybeare, Frederick C.; Harris, James R.; Lewis, Agnes S.
    1898   *The Story of Aḥiḳar*. London: Clay.

    1913   "The Story of Aḥiḳar." Pp. 715–784 in *The Apocrypha and Pseudepigrapha of the Old Testament*, vol. 2. Ed. R. H. Charles. Oxford: Clarendon.

Cowley, Arthur E.
    1923   *Aramaic Papyri of the Fifth Century B.C.* Oxford: Clarendon.

Denis, Albert M.
    1970   *Introduction aux pseudépigraphes grecs d'Ancien Testament.* SVTP 1. Leiden: Brill.

Kraft, Robert A., ed.
    1974   *The Testament of Job.* SBLTT, Pseudepigrapha Series 4. Missoula: SBL/Scholars.

Moore, Carey A.
    1977   *Daniel, Esther and Jeremiah: The Additions.* AB 44. Garden City, NY: Doubleday.

Philonenko, Marc
    1958   "Le *Testament de Job* et les Thérapeutes." *Semitica* 8:41–53.

Torrey, Charles C.
    1946   *The Lives of the Prophets*. JBLMS 1. Philadelphia: SBL.

THE PRONOUNCEMENT STORY IN PHILO AND JOSEPHUS

Leonard Greenspoon
Clemson University

ABSTRACT

Pronouncement stories are rare in the extensive writings of Philo and Josephus. The one exception to this statement is Philo's treatise *Every Good Man Is Free*. In almost all cases in Philo the characters in pronouncement stories come from Greek history or mythology, rather than from the Jewish world. In the few pronouncement stories in Josephus, Jewish figures and concerns do appear, but Josephus, like Philo, does not use the pronouncement story to place striking utterances in the mouths of outstanding leaders of Biblical and Jewish history.

0.1   Philo and Josephus, Jewish writers at the opposite ends of the first century A.D., are important figures in any study of Judaism or early Christianity. In common with many authors of antiquity, they wrote a great deal. What is remarkable in their case, and this serves to enhance their importance, is the fact that so much of what they wrote has survived (for the most part preserved in Christian circles). Their writings are conveniently accessible in the Loeb Classical Library, where the works of Philo are published in twelve volumes and the works of Josephus in nine /1/.

While Josephus is most famous for his histories and Philo for his philosophical allegorical treatises, both writers employed a number of genres to achieve their respective goals. They are also similar in that each was at the same time an original thinker and the preserver and synthesizer of traditions inherited from a variety of Jewish and non-Jewish sources.

0.2   All of the above are features making it likely that here one will find numerous examples of forms such as the pronouncement story, for the combined corpus is extensive, varied, and the product of original reflection on heterogeneous traditional material. That this is not the case, that in fact pronouncement stories are, with but one exception, not characteristic of the writings of Philo and Josephus, is a significant, if negative, finding. I think that it is worth presenting the evidence from these two writers, even though—

or precisely because—it is largely negative. After I have discussed the relatively few examples of pronouncement stories, pointing out unique as well as common features, I will present, in necessarily tentative form, a few suggestions to account for the meager results of my search.

1.   Philo

1.1   I have detected 17 pronouncement stories in the Philonic corpus (listed by book and paragraph in order of their appearance in the Loeb edition): *Cherubim* 63; *Unchangeableness* 146; *Planter* 65, 80; *Abraham* 260f.; *Every Good Man Is Free (EGMIF)* 93–95, 102f., 115, 121f., 122, 123, 124, 125, 127–130, 144, 157; *Providence* 29f. Immediately apparent is the fact that more than half of these examples (11 out of 17) are bunched together in the last third of one treatise, *Every Good Man Is Free*. As we shall see, that pattern of distribution is closely linked to another phenomenon: almost all of Philo's pronouncement stories deal with characters from Greek history or mythology, and not with Jewish figures from the Biblical or later periods.

1.2   According to Colson's introduction to this treatise (found in volume IX of the Loeb edition, pp. 2–9), *Every Good Man Is Free*, "usually believed to be a youthful essay of Philo's," is "an argument to show the truth of the Stoic 'paradox' that the wise man alone is free." Colson also points to the fact that there are in this treatise "only five allusions to or quotations from the Pentateuch," in contrast to "the great preponderance of secular illustration." This "secular illustration," apart from a lengthy section on the Essenes, is for the most part contained in vignettes drawn from the Greek world: the Indian Calanus corrects Alexander the Great (93–95); the slave Heracles appears to respond to the objections of his owner by disdainfully ignoring them (102f.); Dardanian women, taken prisoners by the Macedonians, display exemplary action in a difficult situation when they choose to drown their children rather than allow them to live as slaves (although there is no doubt that this paragraph, which ends with a saying on the part of the mothers, is a pronouncement story, it is difficult to determine its type) (115); the philosopher Diogenes fearlessly corrects the "preposterous" behavior of his captors (121f.), more gently corrects a dejected fellow captive through the apt quotation of a passage from Homer (122), asserts his "freedom, nobility, and natural kingliness" in the face of prospective purchasers (in an inquiry or testing inquiry) (123), offers a pointed correction to an effeminate would-be purchaser that causes the latter to "subside" (124), and deflates the ballooning ego of "one of the so-called freedmen [who was] pluming himself" in yet another correction story (157); in like manner, Chaereas, "a man of culture," corrects the threatening Ptolemy through a quotation from Homer (125); Theodorus, "surnamed the atheist," provides verbose responses (which one cannot help feeling were characteristic of him) to objections raised on account of his previous banishment from Athens (127–130); finally, Antigenidas the flute-player comes out with a witty, brief retort to correct the presumptions of a rival (144).

1.21   In looking over these stories, one notices first of all that Diogenes (a favorite elsewhere as well; see Diogenes Laertius, *Lives of Eminent Philosophers VI* 20–81) is the main character in almost half of these stories. It is also noteworthy that the element of correction is predominant, and this not only in narratives we can classify as correction stories. There is nothing particularly Jewish in all of this; in fact, it would be hard to imagine a Biblical hero uttering some of these statements. Overall, one gets the impression that here Philo strung together a series of accounts, some of which were already in the form of the pronouncement story, embedding them in a minimal amount of introductory or explanatory material. While the ancient understanding of authorship is sufficiently elastic to allow us to term Philo the "author" of this section, it might be more appropriate to speak of him here as an editor or anthologist.

1.3   The general impressions gained from our investigation of the material in *Every Good Man Is Free* are for the most part confirmed when we look at the other six examples from Philo. The story recounted in *Cherubim* 63 is like the previous ones in that the main (here, the only) character is from the Greek world, Alexander the Great (see also *EGMIF* 93–95). It differs from those summarized above in its classification, for this is a (self-) commendation story. Nevertheless, as Philo uses this narrative it does serve to correct the words of the king, who is shown by his own utterance to be foolish.

1.31   In two different treatises, *Unchangeableness* and *Planter*, Philo tells the same story about Socrates (who remains unnamed in the Philonic text). Since these correction stories are short, I want to give both of them in their entirety:

> There is a story that one of the ancients beholding a gaily decked and costly pageant turned to some of his disciples and said to them, "My friends, observe how many things there are I do not need." *Unchangeableness* 146

> They say that in olden time one who was enraptured by the beauty of wisdom, as by that of some distinguished lady, after watching the array of a procession pass by on which vast sums had been lavished, fastened his eyes on a group of his associates and said, "See, my friends, of how many things I have no need." *Planter* 65

The saying attributed to Socrates is worded identically in both passages (only the position of the vocative differs); however, we note that Philo paints a slightly more expansive picture of the setting in his use of this narrative in *Planter*. This indicates that Philo did on occasion modify pronouncement stories that he incorporated into his text in accordance with the context in which he placed them.

1.32   The wisdom of Socrates is represented through another pronouncement story in the treatise *Planter*. Here (*Planter* 80) the sage, again unnamed
in Philo's text, appears to correct the general understanding of wisdom by
declaring that "he was the only man who knew that he knew nothing." The
second fragment of the treatise *On Providence* contains a pronouncement story
that narrates how, through both action and words, the elder Dionysius, tyrant
of Syracuse, corrected Damocles' (not named in Philo) false impression that
the ruler's life was a happy one (*Providence* 29f.).

1.33   A Biblical leader figures in the pronouncement stories of Philo only
in *Abraham* 260f., and here—it is important to note—not as the person who
speaks but as the individual spoken about. The "chief men of the country,"
upon viewing the "quiet sober air of sorrow pervading" Abraham's house at
the time of his mourning over the death of Sarah, were led to exclaim: "Thou
art a king from God among us." This account then is to be classified as a
laudation, i.e., as a subtype of the commendation in which the main character
is the commended one rather than the one commending.

1.4   In summary, it is clear that for Philo the pronouncement story is
neither a frequently used nor a highly developed form. In 16 out of 17 cases
Philo seems to have taken into his text, with little or no modification,
pronouncement stories that were circulating through the Greek world and that
were also used by earlier, contemporary, and later writers. Few of these
display distinctive Jewish concerns, although Philo did manage to adapt those
narratives (outside of *EGMIF*) that occur in discussions of Biblical material to
their newly-imposed surroundings. In only one case does a Jewish figure
appear, and even here he is allotted no dialogue. Was there a reluctance on
Philo's part, in what is probably the only pronouncement story that he himself
developed, to place an utterance at once striking and forceful in the mouth of a
Biblical hero, a reluctance not felt in connection with spokesmen from the non-
Jewish world?

2.   Josephus

2.1   The pronouncement stories contained in the writings of Josephus
total only nine, approximately half the number found in Philo: *Apion* 1.201–
204; *War* 1.91f., 1.272, 1.651–653, 3.207–210, 6.409–411; *Antiq.* 11.300f.,
12.210–214, 18.174f. No pattern of distribution is immediately apparent from
this list, although those familiar with the *Antiquities* might note that no
pronouncement stories are set in any period prior to the time of Persian
domination. As the discussion that follows makes clear, in only one of
Josephus' pronouncement stories are Jewish figures or concerns absent. This
stands in contrast to the stories in Philo, who, however, shares with Josephus
the tendency to highlight the element of correction. If we were led to conclude
that Philo developed few of his pronouncement stories on his own, the opposite

conclusion can be reached with respect to many of the accounts found in Josephus. Is it for this reason that we gain the overall impression that the narratives in Josephus are frequently less clear as to type, less pointed, and therefore less successful as pronouncement stories?

2.2   For the pronouncement story found at *Apion* 1.201–204, Josephus explicitly states that his source was the Greek historian Hecataeus. In this narrative, which is one in a lengthy series of accounts provided by Josephus to prove the antiquity of the Jews on the basis of non-Jewish sources, a Jewish soldier Mosollamus corrects the view of Alexander's soldiers that the observation of birds should figure in military strategy by both shooting the bird and answering subsequent objections to such "impious" behavior:

> Why so mad, you poor wretches? . . . Pray, how could any sound information about our march be given by this creature, which could not provide for its own safety? Had it been gifted with divination, it would not have come to this spot, for fear of being killed by the arrow of Mosollamus the Jew.

2.3   The pronouncement stories contained in the *Jewish War*, all of which seem to have been composed by Josephus himself, are not on the whole as clearly defined or striking as the narrative taken up by Josephus from Hecataeus. They cover the following topics: the subjects of Alexander Jannaeus provide a harsh corrective to their ruler's hope that a simple change of policy would placate them when they declare that he could "pacify them" only with his own death (1.91f.); the dying Phasael appears to correct a false sense of security on the part of his foe Antigonus by reference to the escape of his brother Herod (1.272); a group of youths, who were soon to die because they had dared to cut down the golden eagle erected by Herod over the great gate of the Jerusalem temple, courageously respond to that dying king's objections (1.651–653); the Roman general Vespasian tries to make a virtue of necessity when he urges his soldiers to resist being drawn into combat that was proving unsuccessful against Jewish forces sallying forth from the besieged town of Jotapata (this narrative, rather lengthy in both setting and response, is a correction story) (3.207–210); Titus, entering the defeated city of Jerusalem, commends the strength of that city's towers and especially the God of Israel, who indeed "has been with us in the war." It was God "who brought down the Jews from these strongholds; for what power have human hands or machines against these towers?" (6.409–411).

2.4   The three pronouncement stories found in the *Jewish Antiquities* are quite varied in subject matter and form: in the first Bagōsēs, general of the Persian ruler Artaxerxes, responds tellingly to Jewish objections to his entering into the Jerusalem temple by querying whether he was not in fact purer than Jēsūs, brother of the high priest Jōannēs, whom the high priest had slain in the temple itself (11.300f.); the Tobiad Hyrcanus corrects the impression made by a heap of bones, stacked in front of his place at the banquet table of Ptolemy by his rivals, through a descriptive reference to the habits of dogs (12.210–214); the emperor Tiberius, when reproached for his habit of allowing governors and procurators to remain at their posts until they died (some felt that short-term appointments or frequent replacements were preferable), responded with a "fable by way of illustration": a wounded man rebuffs the attempts of a passer-by to shoo away the swarm of flies that appeared to be plaguing him by noticing that

> since these flies have already had their fill of blood, they no longer feel such a pressing need to annoy me but are in some measure slack. But if others were to come with a fresh appetite, they would take over my weakened body and that would indeed be the death of me. (18.174f.)

The last story is the only one which has no particular connection with Judaism.

2.5   For Josephus the pronouncement story is no more characteristic a form than it is for Philo. Nevertheless, even in his infrequent use of it Josephus reveals certain differences. Thus Josephus touched upon distinctly Jewish concerns in all but one of his pronouncement stories. Moreover, it is likely that Josephus himself developed the majority of the narratives of this type that he included in his writings. It is worth noting that, for all his concentration on Jewish matters, Josephus did not put any of the utterances in the mouth of Biblical or later Jewish heroes. In this his practice is identical to that of Philo.

2.51   In neither Philo nor Josephus are Biblical leaders mute; their words, whether one sentence remarks or lengthy addresses, are simply not preserved, in these two writers at least, in the form of the pronouncement story. On occasion, however, such utterances do occur in something that approaches the pronouncement story. This is the case, for example, at the following places: for Josephus, in *Antiq.* 6.155, where Samuel replies sharply to Agag, king of the Amalekites, whom Saul had spared; for Philo, in *Flight* 140, where it is God Himself who replies encouragingly to Moses. Josephus is paraphrasing a Biblical scene that contains a striking saying, and Philo has reduced a Biblical dialogue to a single question and answer in order to make a point. It is doubtful that either passage would have circulated as a complete and independent story.

3.   Having surveyed all of the examples that I located in both Philo and Josephus, I wish finally to consider some of the factors whose interplay produced the situation I have described. Let us look first at what I call literary factors. Thus, Josephus and Philo, both of whom allowed themselves to develop their arguments and themes at length, had no need to make frequent use of a form which compresses much into a relatively few words. Josephus,

more than Philo, composed a few pronouncement stories of his own, but neither lavished the care or effort on this form that they did on certain others. The same would hold true for many of the sources upon which these two writers drew, for it is not likely that as a rule they would go out of their way to transform relevant pronouncement stories they came upon into something else (Philo, *Every Good Man Is Free*, supports this point).

3.1   Still, I find that not all questions can be answered by the appeal to literary factors. This is especially so when we consider again the fact that in no pronouncement story that I have found, with the possible exception of Josephus, *Antiq.* 6.155, does the choice and striking statement, and the sense of authority that often goes with it, belong to a well-known Jewish leader from the Biblical or post-Biblical period. In this Philo and Josephus reflect a factor, perhaps a theological factor, that influenced both their sources and their own thinking. Sources dealing with the Greek world were not reluctant to attribute striking and authoritative statements in the form of pronouncement stories to mythological and historical heroes, and Jewish authors such as Philo and Josephus included relevant examples of these stories in their writings. It seems that their sources on Jewish history did not embed the statements of Jewish leaders in similar stories, and Josephus and Philo did not use this form to frame their own accounts of the words of past or contemporary Jewish leaders. Is there implicit in all of this the feeling that the particular authority that would adhere to prominent Jewish spokesmen whose teachings on distinctive Jewish concerns were preserved in the form of the pronouncement story represented an encroachment by humans upon a sphere properly reserved for God alone? In other words, it was appropriate for non-Jews, when they dealt with general concerns or even recognized the unique power of the God of Israel, to receive the emphasis accorded to the main speaker in a pronouncement story; it was likewise acceptable for an individual Jew or group of Jews to make an occasional observation; however, it was inappropriate to accord undue prominence to past or contemporary Jewish leaders, whose statements gained authority not through any particularity of person or situation, but through the convergence of human utterance with the divine will.

3.2   The preceding two paragraphs, and especially the second one, are admittedly speculative. Nevertheless, the observation that Philo and Josephus, two first-century writers who are in many respects markedly different, share certain basic characteristics in their infrequent use of the pronouncement story invites one to explore the reasons why this is so. I have succumbed to this tempting invitation and urge others to feel free to do likewise.

NOTE

/1/   The translation of Philo is by F. H. Colson, G. H. Whitaker, and Ralph Marcus; the translation of Josephus is by H. St. J. Thackeray, Ralph Marcus, and L. H. Feldman. These translations are used in the quotations below.

WORKS CONSULTED

Josephus
    1961ff.   *Josephus.* 9 vols. Loeb Classical Library. Cambridge, MA: Harvard
                       University.

Philo
    1956ff.   *Philo.* 12 vols. Loeb Classical Library. Cambridge, MA: Harvard
                       University.

THE PRONOUNCEMENT STORY IN TANNAITIC LITERATURE: A REVIEW OF BULTMANN'S THEORY

Gary G. Porton
University of Illinois

ABSTRACT

This paper reviews Bultmann's ideas concerning the relationship between the *apophthegmata* of the Gospels and rabbinic literature. Because Bultmann did not limit his inquiry into the rabbinic texts to the Tannaitic stratum, many of his examples are irrelevant to his concerns. This paper presents the results of a search for Tannaitic passages which are similar to the *apophthegmata* of the Gospels. It argues that there are few pericopae in the Tannaitic collections which serve as good parallels to the pronouncement stories found in the Gospels. This essay suggests that we find relatively few *apophthegmata* in the Tannaitic stratum because the editors of these documents lacked the concern for the personality of their sages which was present for the authors of the Gospels. The paper finally suggests that the best parallels to the *apophthegmata* of the Gospels are found in the Greek literature on the philosophers and politicians.

0.   Introduction

0.1   This paper is an assessment of Bultmann's views about the relationship of the *apophthegmata* in the Gospels to Palestinian rabbinic literature. Although the essay contains a number of pericopae from Tannaitic collections, I have not offered detailed literary analyses of these passages. Such discussions would entail comparisons of parallel versions, evaluations of textual variants, and detailing of the contexts in which these passages appear. While the results of such investigations would be important, some conclusions concerning Bultmann's views can be reached without them.

0.2   This study was undertaken as part of a joint project of the Pronouncement Story Work Group of the Society of Biblical Literature. Originally, Professor W. Sibley Towner and I shared responsibility for the rabbinic texts. Unfortunately, Professor Towner had to withdraw from the group in 1977. Before withdrawing, however, he submitted a summary of

his research up to September, 1976. I wish to express the debt of the present
essay to Professor Towner's preliminary studies.

1.   Bultmann's Theory

1.1   Bultmann saw a close relationship between the *apophthegmata* he
found in the Gospels and "rabbinic literature." He argued that the "controversy dialogues" are closely paralleled in the rabbinic texts: "To carry on dis-
putes in this way is typically *Rabbinic*" (41). He cites Lev. R. 34:3, M. A. Z.
3:4, M. Ber. 2:5, M. Ber. 2:6, ARN 4, and b. Beṣ. 63a as rabbinic prototypes of
the controversy and scholastic dialogues (42). He states, "Rabbinic controversy
and scholastic dialogues . . . find their starting-point . . . in some particular
occasion. . . . The typical form for an answer is the *counter-question*, and
often it appears in such a form as to be a metaphor in form, too. Sometimes
instead of the metaphor the counter-question is a detailed *parable*, . . . inter-
rogatory in character" (42). Bultmann selects "a few examples from the abun-
dant material": Mid. Qoh. 1:7, b. Shab. 119a, Ex. R. 30, b. A. Z. 54bMekh. Ish.
Jethro 6, b. Sanh. 90b, b. Tan. 7a, b. Sanh. 39a, Num. R. 3:2, Pesiq. R. 21, b.
Hul. 59b, Mid. Qoh. 8:17, b. A. Z. 10a, Lev. R. 4, Gen. R. 4, b. Ber. 8b (42–45).
In summation Bultmann writes: "One has only to review such examples as
these to see clearly that the same kind of argument is found here as there,
among the Rabbis as in the Synoptic controversy dialogues" (45).

1.2   Concerning the "scholastic dialogues" Bultmann writes that "in
view of the close relationship between the scholastic and the controversy
dialogues, little needs to be said about the construction of the former. . . .
Rabbinic stories offer parallels here, too, as we have already seen" (54).

1.3   Bultmann again turns to rabbinic stories when he considers "the
origin of biographical apophthegms," for "they offer parallels in profusion"
(57). Bultmann cites the following rabbinic texts as relevant parallels to the
biographical *apophthegmata*: Mid. Qoh. 9:7, b. Yoma 87a, b. Tan. 20a, Tos.
Pes. 1:27, b. Sanh. 105b, Gen. R. 11, b. Sanh. 101a, b. Ber. 28b, Lev. R. 34:3,
M. A. Z. 2:7, M. Avot 2:6, Lev. R. 3, b. Ber. 33a, b. Mak. 24a-b (57–59) /1/.
In summary he writes that "after all this there can be no doubt that
biographical apophthegms, like the others, have their parallels in Rabbinic
tradition" (60).

1.4   From Bultmann's comments, one would expect to find a large
number of relevant parallels in the rabbinic collections to the *apophthegmata* Bultmann described in the Gospels. The following comments will
demonstrate, however, that this is not the case. In fact, given the extent of
the relevant rabbinic documents, there are surprisingly few good parallels to
the Gospel materials.

2.   General Criticism of Bultmann's Method

2.1   Bultmann's method of comparing the materials from the Gospels
to the rabbinic documents can be challenged at two major points. First, he
relied heavily on secondary sources rather than original texts. The biases of
the works on which he based his work and the organization of these studies
affected Bultmann's selection of material /2/. Second, like the scholars on
whom he relied, Bultmann did not distinguish between early and late
rabbinic collections /3/. It was unimportant to him that the majority of the
examples he cited came from documents edited centuries after the Gospels
had reached their completion (see Porton, 1976:4).

2.2   Bultmann's failure to limit his search for rabbinic parallels to the
Gospel material to the Tannaitic stratum is his most serious methodological
flaw. Tannaitic literature comprises those documents which were edited
before the middle of the third century C.E. If we wish to find in rabbinic
literature those passages which are relevant to a discussion of the Gospels,
we must select our texts from those rabbinic collections which are most
closely contemporaneous to the Gospels. We know that the literary forms of
rabbinic pericopae are influenced by many factors. One important factor is
the document in which a passage appears (see Porton, 1981: Chap. 2). A
pericope may be cast in one literary pattern in one collection and in another
form in a different text. Elsewhere, I have discussed a literary pattern which
occurs only in the Palestinian *gemara*. I have shown that when a pericope
set in this form in the Palestinian Talmud appears in other collections it is
cast in a literary pattern appropriate to those collections (Porton, 1978).
Because the issue before us is, in general terms, the literary form in which a
saying is placed in the document, and we know that the date of a document
affects the forms it contains, we should seek rabbinic parallels to the Gospel
material with care. Finding parallels to Gospel stories in seventh century
documents tells us little about the material available to the writers of the
Gospels. Some may argue that Amoraic documents /4/ contain Tannaitic
materials. This line of reasoning, however, begs the question. The issue
before us is not only the sayings but also the forms in which they have been
set. Enough work has been done in the area of literary analysis of rabbinic
literature by Professor Jacob Neusner of Brown University and others that it
is beyond doubt that later editors often reformulated materials which
reached them (Neusner, 1970, 1971, 1973). To my mind it is impossible to
sustain the argument that the Amoraic texts contain earlier material which
has remained unchanged from the Tannaitic period. As Towner writes,
"Considering the difficulty in recovering both the form and content even of
Tannaitic traditions from any period prior to 70 A.D. (a difficulty demonstrated recently and in detail by Neusner and his Brown associates), the

eliciting of 'parallels' to a NT *Gattung* from Talmudic and later sources would appear to be highly anachronistic" (2).

2.3   In order to bring to light those passages in the rabbinic collections which are relevant to the Gospel materials, the passages cited in this paper are drawn exclusively from Mishnah, Tosefta, Sifra, Sifré, and the Mekhilta of Rabbi Ishmael. I have not used any source whose Tannaitic character is not firmly established, such as Mekhilta of Rabbi Simeon b. Yoḥai, Sifré Zuṭṭa, Midrash Tannaim, or the *baraitot*. Treating the *baraitot* presents the most problems, for it generally has been assumed that those sections in the *gemarot* designated as *baraitot* are from the Tannaitic period. However, recent studies by Neusner and others (see Goodblatt: *passim*) have shown that many of the *baraitot* are Amoraic creations, or at best, Amoraic re-workings of earlier Tannaitic sources. Because the Tannaitic character of each *baraita* must be demonstrated individually, I have decided not to include this material in the present inquiry.

3.   The Tannaitic Material

3.1   The first set of Tannaitic passages are to my mind the best parallels to the accounts in the Gospels. The rabbinic pericopae contain specific information about the setting in which the principal pronouncement was uttered (as do most of the Gospel *apophthegmata*), the principal pronouncement is assigned to a named sage, it responds to a question, statement, or phenomenon encountered by the sage, and it is not part of a dialogue between equals.

> M. Avot 2:6: Also he [Hillel] saw one skull floating on the face of the water. He said to it: "Because you drowned [others], they drowned you, and in the end, they that drowned you shall be drowned."

This passage occurs in a list of short sayings attributed to Hillel. It is the only saying in the list which is occasioned by Hillel's encountering a particular phenomenon; that is, it is the only statement which is placed in a particular setting. Furthermore, it is the only comment which does not have a generalized moral or legal import. Both Neusner (1971: III, 59) and Bultmann (59) cite this as a Jewish pronouncement story. It seems to me to be a good parallel to some of the material in the Gospels.

> Sifré Deut. 305: And one time R. Yoḥanan b. Zakkai was riding on a donkey, and his students were walking after him. He saw one young woman plucking grain from under the feet of an Arab's cow. When she saw R. Yoḥanan b. Zakkai, she wrapped herself in her hair and stood before him. She said to him: "Rabbi, provide [food] for me." He said to her: "Whose daughter are you?" She said to him: "I am the daughter of Naqdimon b. Goryon." She said to him: "Rabbi, remember when you signed my marriage contract [as a witness]?" R. Yoḥanan b. Zakkai said to his students: "I signed this one's marriage contract, and I read in it a thousand gold *dinars* of her father-in-law's house. [I also remember that members of] this young

girl's house did not enter to worship on the Holy Mount until they spread for them a cloth of fine wool under their feet. [Then] they would enter, worship, and return to their homes happy. All my days I sought [the meaning] of this verse but I did not find it: *If you do not know this, O loveliest of women, follow the tracks of the flock and take your kids to graze close by the shepherds' tents* (Cant. 1:8). Do not read *your kids* (gdywtyk) but 'your body (gwywtyk),' for all the time that Israel does the will of the Omnipresent no nation nor kingdom [can] rule over her. But when Israel does not do the will of the Omnipresent, He delivers her into the hand of a lowly nation. And not [only] into the hand of a lowly nation but [also] under the feet of the cattle of the lowly nation."

Yoḥanan's saying, which appears here as an exegetical remark, was occasioned by his seeing the woman plucking the grain from under the Arab's cow and by his remembering that she came from a wealthy family. Neusner (1970:21) states: "The pericope is obviously a composite of two separate components. The first is the meeting with the girl. The second is the exegesis of Song 1:8 for which the meeting provides the setting."

There are a number of full and partial parallels to the version in Sifré Deut. In Mekh. Ish. *Bahodesh* 1, Yoḥanan's interpretation of the verse is considerably different from the one before us. In Mekh. Ish. he states:

"*If you do not know this, O loveliest of women.* You did not want to serve Heaven, behold, [now] you serve the lowliest of nations, [the] Arabs. You did not want to pay the head tax to heaven, *a beqa a head* (Ex. 38:26), behold, [now] you pay a head tax of fifteen *sheqels* under the government of your enemies. You did not want to repair the roads and streets going up to [the Temple], behold, [now] you repair the posts and stations [on the roads] going up to the royal cities."

The formulation of the two interpretations is quite different. The former is more generalized, and, to my mind, makes a stronger point. It is important to remember that both of these examples are taken from Tannaitic documents. The formulation of the story differs from the account on b. Ket. 66b, which is cited as a *baraita* (Neusner, 1970:235–237).

Mekh. Ish. Vayassa' 1: Again it once happened that one student went [before the ark to lead the service] in the presence of R. Eliezer, and [the student] lengthened his prayers. [Eliezer]'s students said to him: "Our rabbi, you saw that so-and-so lengthened his prayers." . . . [Eliezer] said to them: "He did not lengthen [them] more than Moses, for it is said: *So I fell down before the Lord forty days . . .*" (Deut. 9:25). For R. Eliezer used to say: "There is a time to shorten [one's prayers] and a time to lengthen [them]."

A similar story in which the student shortens his prayers immediately precedes this passage; therefore, Eliezer's last statement applies to both cases. As the pericope now stands, the principal pronouncement follows "for R. Eliezer used to say." The form of this introduction suggests that the statement was not originally attached to this story. And, in fact, we do find the comment independent of this story (Neusner, 1973:26–28). By connecting the statement to this setting, the editor has placed Eliezer's comment in a particular setting.

Mekh. Ish. Pisḥa 16: One time the students spent the Sabbath in Yavneh but R. Joshua [could] not spend the Sabbath there. When his students came to him, he said to them: "What new things [did] you [learn] in Yavneh?" They said to him: "After you, Rabbi." He said to them: "And who spent the Sabbath there?" They said to him: "R. Eleazar b. ʿAzzariah." He said to them: "Is it possible that R. Eleazar b. ʿAzzariah spent the Sabbath there and you [did] not [learn] anything new!" They said to him: "[He stated] this general statement [when] he explained [Deut. 29:9–10]: 'You are standing today all of you . . . your little ones and your wives. Now, did a little one actually know [enough] to understand [the difference] between good and evil? Rather, [they were mentioned in the verse] to give a reward to those who brought them [and] to increase a reward for those who do His will to establish what is said, *The Lord was pleased for His righteousness' sake*'" (Isa. 42:21). He said to them: "This is a new teaching and more than that, [for] behold I was like a person seventy years old but I was not worthy [to understand] this thing until today. Happy are you Abraham, our father, for Eleazar b. ʿAzzariah came out of your loins. The generation is not an orphan generation, for Eleazar b. ʿAzzariah dwells in it."

Joshua's pronouncement praises Eleazar b. ʿAzzariah. The praise is occasioned by the former's students reporting to their teacher what Eleazar had taught on the previous Sabbath. This pericope has all of the elements of a pronouncement story. Towner (8) also cites this story. Although there are other versions of this passage, they do not differ greatly from the one before us.

M. Ber. 2:5: One time R. Gamliel recited the *Shemaʿ* on the first night of his marriage. His students said to him: "Did you not teach us, our Rabbi, that the groom is exempt from reciting the *Shemaʿ* on the first night of his marriage?" He said to them: "I will not listen to you so that I would remove the Kingdom of Heaven from me for even one hour!"

M. Ber. 2:6: [One time R. Gamliel] washed on the first night after his wife had died. His students said to him: "Did you not teach us, our Rabbi, that a mourner is forbidden to wash?" He said to them: "I am not like other men, for I am ill."

M. Ber. 2:7: And when Tabi his slave died, [R. Gamliel] received consolation because of him. His students said to him: "Did you not teach us, our Rabbi, that one does not receive consolation on account of slaves?" He said to them: "Tabi was not like other slaves; he was ritually fit."

The editor of the second chapter of M. Ber. clearly saw the similaritie among these three stories, for he grouped them together. In each case Gamliel's comment responds to his students' question. Each question i occasioned by the fact that Gamliel seems not to be following his owɪ teaching. As Professor Tannehill stated to me, the accusation that Jesus is no living according to his own teachings does not appear in the synoptic pro nouncement stories. The nature of the first comment differs from the othe two. In M. Ber. 2:5 Gamliel explains his action is a result of his not wantinɡ to lose any chance of reciting the *shemaʿ* and thereby receiving the King dom of Heaven. His other two justifications are of a less "religious character. Bultmann (42) cites the first two passages; however, the third passage seems to me to be equally relevant.

> *M. Ber. 1:1:* One time [R. Gamliel]'s sons returned [after midnight] from a wedding feast. They said to him: "We have not recited the *Shemaʿ* ." He said to them: "If the morning star has not risen, you are obligated to recite it."

In this passage, Gamliel's comment, which is of a legal nature, grows out of a particular setting. He stated it in response to his sons' remark. The legal nature of the comment differs from the Gospel material; however, this pericope does have certain affinities with the pronouncement story. It is highly unusual for a legal statement to be given in a specific setting. The passage opens with "one time" (m ʿ šh b), which is often found as the introduction to passages in the Tannaitic corpus that are similar to the pronouncement stories in the Gospels. Towner (4) also draws attention to this passage /5/.

> *Tos. Ḥag. 2:1:* One time R. Yoḥanan b. Zakkai was riding on his donkey, and R. Leazar b. ʿArak was close behind him. [Leazar] said to him: "Rabbi, teach me one section of the *Maʿaśeh Merkavah.*" [Yoḥanan] said to him: "No! Thus I have said to you previously that they do not teach about the *Merkavah* to an individual unless he is a sage who understands his own knowledge." [Leazar] said to him: "Now I wish to discuss with you." [Yoḥanan] said to him: "Speak!" R. Leazar b. ʿArak opened [his discourse] and expounded the *Maʿaśeh Merkavah.* R. Yoḥanan b. Zakkai got down from his donkey and wrapped himself in his prayer shawl, and both of them sat on a stone under an olive tree, and he discussed before him. [Yoḥanan] stood and kissed him on his head and said: "Blessed is the Lord, the God of Israel, who gave a son to Abraham, our father, who knows [how] to understand and to explain the glory of our Father in heaven. There are those who expound well but do not live well. There are those who live well but do not expound well. But Leazar b. ʿArak expounds well and lives well. Happy are you, Abraham our father, for Leazar b. ʿArak, who knows [how] to understand and to explain the glory of our Father in heaven, came out of your loins."

Yoḥanan's praise of Leazar is occasioned by the latter's ability to correctly explain the mysteries of the Chariot. Yoḥanan's praise of Leazar is rather long. In some of the other versions of this story Yoḥanan's comment is considerably shorter (Neusner, 1970:66–68, 247–251).

> *Tos. Shebu. 3:6:* One time R. Reuben spent the Sabbath in Tiberias, and one philosopher found him. He said to him: "Which is one who is hated in the world?" [Reuben] said to him: "The one who denies his Creator." [The philosopher] said to him: "How [does he deny Him]?" [Reuben] said to him: "*Honor your father and your mother. Do not murder. Do not commit adultery. Do not steal. Do not bear false witness against your neighbor. Do not covet.* Behold, a man does not deny a thing until he denies [its] essential point. And a man commits a sin only after he has denied [the existence] of the One who commanded concerning it."

This is a fairly good parallel to the Gospel material. R. Reuben's comment is a response to the philosopher's question.

Tos. Nid. 5:15: It happened to Hananyah b. Hananyah that his father dedicated him to be a Nazirite. He brought him before R. Gamliel, [and] R. Gamliel examined him to see if he were of age. [Hananyah] said to him: "Why are you worried? [Are you worried that] I am [not] under my father's authority? [If] I am under my father's authority, behold, I am a Nazirite. But if I am under my own authority, I am a Nazirite from this moment [forward." Gamliel] stood and kissed him on the head. He said: "I am certain that you will be an authoritative teacher in Israel before you die." And he did become an authoritative teacher in Israel before his death.

In this pericope Gamliel praises Hananyah. Gamliel's praise results from the fact that Hananyah was willing to fulfill his father's wish that he become a Nazirite whether or not his father had control over Hananyah's life. This passage has all the elements of a pronouncement story.

Tos. Pisha 4:13: One time the 14th [of Nisan] fell on the Sabbath. They asked Hillel the Elder: "Does the Passover offering override the Sabbath?" He said to them: "And do we have only one Passover offering in the year which overrides the Sabbath? We have more than 300 Passover offerings in the year, and they [all] override the Sabbath." The whole courtyard collected against him. He said to them: "The continual offering is a community sacrifice and the Passover offering is a community sacrifice. Just as the continual offering, which is a community sacrifice, overrides the Sabbath, so the Passover offering, which is a community sacrifice, overrides the Sabbath. Another matter: It is said concerning the continual offering, *its season* (Num. 28:2), and *its season* (Num. 9:2) is said concerning the Passover offering. Just as the continual offering, concerning which *its season* is said, overrides the Sabbath, so the Passover offering, concerning which *its season* is said, overrides the Sabbath. And furthermore, [it is an] *a fortiori* [argument]: Although the continual offering, which does not produce the liability of [the punishment of] cutting off, overrides the Sabbath, the Passover offering, which does produce the liability of [the punishment of] cutting off, how much the more should it override the Sabbath. And further, I have received from my masters [the tradition] that the Passover offering overrides the Sabbath, and not [merely] the first Passover offering [overrides the Sabbath] but [also] the second [Passover offering], and not [merely] the Passover offering of the community but [also] the Passover offering of the individual [overrides the Sabbath]." They said to him: "What will be the rule for the people who do not bring knives and Passover offerings to the Sanctuary [on the Sabbath]?" He said to them: "Leave them alone, the holy spirit is upon them. If they are not prophets, they are the disciples of prophets."

It is obvious that this passage is composed of a number of different elements. Neusner (1971:II, 231–236, 286–289) has analyzed this passage and compared the different versions. Hillel's bringing such a large number of arguments to meet the objections of those in the courtyard is not paralleled in the Gospels, nor is it a common procedure in the rabbinic pericopae. As Neusner notes (1971:II, 231–236), Hillel's opinion is not accepted until he quotes the teaching of his masters. Neusner (1971:III, 59) argues that Hillel's last statement is an *apophthegma*. The saying is set in a narrative setting, and it responds to a direct question.

Tos. Kel. B. B. 1:2–3: One time one woman who had woven a garment in cleanness came before R. Ishmael for [him] to examine her. She said to him: "Rabbi, I know that the garment was not rendered unclean; however, it was not in my heart to guard it [from uncleanness]." As a result of the examination of her which R. Ishmael conducted, she said to him: "Rabbi, I know that a menstrual woman entered and pulled the cord [so that she may have conveyed uncleanness to the garment by her shaking the web] with me." Said R. Ishmael: "How great are the words of the sages, for they used to say: 'If one did not intend to guard it [from uncleanness], it is unclean.'"

A similar story follows this one in all of the documents (Porton, 1976:186–191). In both stories, Ishmael praises the wisdom of the sages. His praise is occasioned by his examination of the women, which confirms in his mind the truth of the sages' comment.

Sifra 45c: It once happened that one of his students was rendering decisions in his presence. [R. Eliezer] said to his wife, Imma Shalom: "He will no longer live after the end of the Sabbath." And when he died after the Sabbath, [the] sages entered and said to [Eliezer], "Rabbi, you are a prophet." He said to them: "I am neither a prophet nor the son of a prophet. However, thus I received from my teachers that anyone who renders *halakhic* decisions in the presence of his teacher deserves death."

This seems to me to be a possible pronouncement story. Eliezer's principal pronouncement is a quotation from his teachers. His comment is occasioned by the sages' comment. There are several versions of this story; in the other accounts Eliezer is named (Neusner, 1973:I, 115).

3.11   These fourteen pericopae are the only passages I have found in the Tannaitic corpus which meet the criteria set forth at the beginning of 3.1. In the following examples, we do not find information about the setting in which the principal comment was uttered. However, we also encounter pronouncements in the Gospels that are not placed in a clear setting, for example, Luke 17: 20–21.

Sifré Deut. 13: *[Choose] wise, understanding, [and experienced] men* (Deut. 1:13). Arios asked this of R. Yosi; he said to him: "Which is a *wise man?*" [Yosi] said to him: "He who makes his learning firm. You say learning or [perhaps one should say] only understanding." [Arios] said to him: "Behold, *understanding men* is already said. What is the [difference] between understanding men and wise men?" [Yosi said to him]: "Wise men are similar to a rich banker. When they bring [him something with which] to see, he sees. When they do not bring [him something with which] to see, he sits and is confounded. Understanding men are similar to a merchant banker. When they do not bring him [something with which] to see, he brings his own things and sees."

Although the Hebrew text is corrupt, this passage seems to me to be similar to a pronouncement story. Yosi's comment is placed in the context of an exegetical debate between him and Arios. Neither the setting in which the debate took place nor the reason for the debate is specified. Yosi's comment is a metaphor. The wise man is one who does not have the resources with which to understand a new teaching on his own. The understanding man is one who can learn new things without the aid of others /6/.

> *Sifra 58b-c*: One student said before R. ʿAqiba: "I must say what I heard [even though it disagrees with what you have taught. *When a woman at childbirth bears a male] she shall be unclean seven days. . . . And on the eighth day [the flesh of his foreskin] shall be circumcised* (Lev. 12:2–3). One might think [that he should be circumcised] fifteen days [after his birth; that is, the] eighth [day after her] seven days [of uncleanness; however,] Scripture says, *on that day*." R. ʿAqiba said to him: "You sink in mighty waters and you bring up clay in your hands, for isn't it already said: *And a son eight days old you shall circumcise, all the males forever*" (Gen. 17:12).

ʿAqiba's principal comment is a rebuke of his student. ʿAqiba's remark is occasioned by his student's exegetical comment; however, the setting in which this exegetical debate took place is not specified.

3.12   The above pericopae offer different types of pronouncement stories. In Mekh. Ish. Pisḥa 16, Tos. Ḥag. 2:1, Tos. Nid. 5:15, and Tos. Kel. B. B. 1:2–3, the pronouncement praises a specific person or a group of persons. The praise is occasioned by a teaching or an action of the one to whom it refers. These are similar to the commendation stories discussed by Tannehill (see 2.2 in his "Introduction" to this volume). In M. Avot 2:6, Sifré Deut. 305, and Mekh. Ish. Vayassaʾl, the sayings are occasioned by the sages' encountering a particular phenomenon, such as a floating skull, the way in which a person recites his prayers, or a woman's plucking grain from under an Arab's cow. Sifré Deut. 305 has some similarities with correction stories (Tannehill, "Introduction," 2.1). Sifra 58b-c is also similar to a correction story, for here ʿAqiba objects to and corrects his student's exegetical remark. M. Ber. 2:5–7 all involve R. Gamliel and his students. In these passages his students question R. Gamliel's actions, which seem to contradict what he had taught them on other occasions. These are similar to objection stories (Tannehill, "Introduction," 2.3). However, the claim that Jesus is not living according to his own teachings is not found in the synoptic pronouncement stories. In M. Ber. 1:1, Tos. Pisḥa 4:13, and Sifré Deut. 13, the principal pronouncements are occasioned by a direct question or an inquiring statement. M. Ber. 1:1 and Tos. Pisḥa 4:13 are similar to inquiry stories (Tannehill, "Introduction," 2.5). Sifra 54c and Sifré Deut. 13 do not seem to me to easily fit into any of Tannehill's categories.

3.2   In the Gospels, the dialogues in which Jesus' pronouncements occur are between unequal parties. However, in the Tannaitic corpus, we find pronouncements appearing in dialogues between equals. This is important, for, as we shall argue below, one of the main goals of the pronouncement stories in the Gospels is to underscore Jesus' unique character.

Sifrē Deut. 38: One time R. Eliezer, R. Joshua, and R. Zadok were reclining at a feast for the son of R. Gamliel. R. Gamliel mixed a glass [of wine] for R. Eliezer, but he did not want to accept [it]. R. Joshua accepted it. R. Eliezer said to him: "What is this, Joshua, for we are reclining and R. Gamliel beRabbi is standing and serving [us]." R. Joshua said to him: "Leave him alone, for Abraham, the great one of the world, served. He served the ministering angels and he thought they were Arabs, idolaters, for it is said, *And he lifted his eyes and saw* . . . (Gen. 18:1). And isn't it an *a fortiori* [argument]? Abraham, the great one of the world, served the ministering angels and he thought they were Arabs, idolaters. Should not R. Gamliel beRabbi serve us? . . . "

There are several versions of this story, and in some of them Zadok offers virtually the same comment as Joshua does here. In some instances, both comments are placed side by side (Neusner, 1973:I, 406–408). The principal pronouncement, which is in the form of a question, is occasioned by Eliezer's refusal to allow Gamliel to serve him.

Sifrē Deut. 43: And one time R. Gamliel, R. Joshua, R. Eleazar b. ʿAzzariah, and R. ʿAqiba entered Rome. They heard a din from Petilon, 120 miles away. They began crying, but R. ʿAqiba laughed. R. ʿAqiba said to them: "Why are you crying?" They said to him: "And you, why are you laughing?" [ʿAqiba] said to them: "And you, why are you crying?" They said to him: "Shouldn't we cry, for the gentiles, idolaters, who offer to [false] gods and prostrate themselves before idols sit in peace and ease. But the House which was the footstool of our God is burned with fire and is the dwelling place for beasts of the field." [ʿAqiba] said to them: "Even so, therefore, I laugh. If [God] acted thus towards those who anger Him, how much the more [will He act thus] towards those who do His will [so that Israel will also eventually dwell in peace and ease]."

This seems to me to have all of the traits of a pronouncement story. ʿAqiba's principal comment is a response to the actions and remarks of his companions. A similar story immediately follows this one, in which ʿAqiba proves that God will eventually bring salvation to Israel and rebuild the Temple. ʿAqiba's remark in this second version is a rather long and complex exegetical statement.

Sifrē Num. 75: *The priests* (Num. 10:8). "Whether blemished or unblemished"— the words of R. Ṭarfon. R. ʿAqiba says: "*Priests* is said here, and *priests* is said elsewhere (Lev. 1:11). Just as *priests* which is said elsewhere [refers to] unblemished [priests] and not to blemished [priests], also here [*priests* refers to] unblemished [priests] and not to blemished [priests]." R. Ṭarfon said to him: "How long will you rake [words] together and bring them against us, ʿAqiba?" He was unable to bear up. "I swear by the life of my children that I saw Simon, my mother's brother, who girded his feet [for he was blemished] standing and blowing the trumpets." [ʿAqiba] said to him: "Yes, [but] perhaps [he did this only] on Rosh HaShanah, Yom Kippur, or the Jubilee year." [Ṭarfon] said to him: "You are not refuted. Happy are you Abraham, our father, for ʿAqiba has come out of your loins. Ṭarfon saw and forgot, [but] ʿAqiba explained [it] on his own and made [it] agree with the *halakhah*. Behold, anyone who separates himself from you [ʿAqiba] it is as if he separated from his own life."

This pericope has all of the traits of a pronouncement story. Ṭarfon's praise of ʿAqiba comes at the end of an exegetical debate. However, the setting or occasion of the debate is not specified.

3.21   I have placed these three pericopae in a separate category because the dialogues are between rabbis of similar or equal status. This feature does not, and cannot, occur in the Gospels, for Jesus' status is unique. Nor does this feature commonly occur in the non-Christian Hellenistic literature. Sifré Deut. 38 and Sifré Deut. 43 are similar to objection stories, and Sifré Num. 75 is similar to a commendation story.

3.3   In the following examples we encounter another unusual feature: the pronouncement is attributed to several people, usually anonymous, or to a single anonymous individual. In these cases, the pronouncements tell us nothing about the character of those who recited them.

> Sifré Deut. 80: One time R. Judah b. Bathyra, R. Mattyah b. Ḥarash, R. Ḥananyah b. Aḥai, R. Joshua, and R. Yonatan were leaving the Land [of Israel]. When they reached Palton, they recalled the Land of Israel, and they stood erect while their eyes shed tears. They rent their garments and recited this verse: "*[You shall indeed cross the Jordan to enter and to make the land your own that the Lord your God is giving you]. You shall possess it and you shall live in it and you must keep and observe all the laws . . .* " (Deut. 11:31). They said: "Living in the Land of Israel is equal to observing all of the [other] commandments [stated] in the Torah."

Following this passage is a similar one in which the same verse and saying are attributed to Eleazar b. Shamoʿa and Yoḥanan the Sandalmaker. Sifré Deut. 80 has two unique features which separate it from the Gospel material. First, the principal pronouncement is placed in the mouth of several people. Second, the pronouncement is occasioned by the actions of those who recited it. There are no other participants in the story, and the actors do not encounter any other phenomena besides their own action. Only the situation in which they find themselves occasions the remark.

> Sifra 94a: One time an ulcer formed on the leg of Joseph b. Pakas, and he asked a doctor to operate. He said to him: "Let me know when [you] finish the operation and [the leg] remains [hanging] as if by a hair." The doctor [finished the operation and] left [the leg hanging] as if by a hair, and he made [this] known to him. [Joseph] called to his son, Naḥunyah. He said to him: "Ḥunyah, my son, until now you have been obligated to care for me. From now on go away, for one does not defile [himself] by the limb of a living person, not even his father's." And when the matter came before the sages, they said that it was said [about him]: "*There is a righteous man that perishes in his righteousness* (Qoh. 7:15), [which means] the righteous one is lost and his righteousness [is lost] with him."

The final pronouncement is an exegetical comment placed in the mouths of the anonymous sages. The occasion for their remarks was their hearing of Joseph's action. The sages object to Joseph's not allowing his son to care for him because the former is overzealous concerning matters of defilement.

The sages argue that one can be, so to speak, too righteous. In this case, the righteousness does no good, for it is lost from the world.

> *Tos. Ber. 3:20:* They said about R. Ḥaninah b. Dosa that he was praying when a lizard bit him; however, he did not stop praying. His students went and found it dead. They said: "Woe to the man whom a lizard bites; woe to the lizard that bites Ben Dosa."

Neusner (1971:III, 59) and Bultmann (59) cite this passage as a rabbinic *apophthegma.* The saying praises Ben Dosa; however, it is uttered by his anonymous students.

> *M. Ber. 1:3:* R. Ṭarfon said: "I was going on the road. I reclined to recite the *Shema'* according to the words of the House of Shammai, and I placed myself in danger from robbers." They said to him: "You deserve to lose your life, for you have transgressed the words of the House of Hillel."

This seems to me to be a pronouncement story. "They" disapprove of Ṭarfon's action when he tells them about it. The principal pronouncement is placed in the mouths of the anonymous "they." The setting in which the debate took place is not specified.

> *Sifrê Deut. 322:* One time [when] Polmos was in Judea, a commander of horsemen ran after an Israelite on a horse in order to kill him, but he did not reach him. Before he reached him a snake bit [the commander] on the heel. [The Israelite] said to him: "Because we are strong, you are delivered into our hands. *Were it not that their Rock had sold them*" (Deut. 32:34).

The principal pronouncement is rather ironic, for it claims that the Israelites were stronger than the Romans, a fact which the events of the day proved incorrect. However, the anonymous Israelite proves his point by citing Deut. 32:34. The Israelites were defeated by the Romans not because the former were weaker than the latter, but because the former had angered God, who had then allowed the Romans to defeat His people.

> *Sifrê Num. 131:* One time Sabta of Ulam hired his donkey to a gentile woman. When she reached the edge of the territory, she said to him: "Wait until I enter the temple of [the territory's] idol." When she came out, he said to her: "Wait for me until I enter and do as you have done." She said to him: "Is it possible that you, a Jew, [will enter and serve the idol]?" He entered [and uncovered himself] and wiped himself on the nose of Peor. Then all the gentiles laughed and said: "Not one man has served [Peor] like this before."

The principal pronouncement is placed in the mouths of the anonymous gentiles. It is occasioned by the fact that Sabta entered the idol's house, defecated, and wiped himself on the idol's nose. Because the account was written by a Jew, he makes the gentiles appear to approve of Sabta's actions.

3.31   With the exception of Sifrê Deut. 80, in these pericopae the principal pronouncement is placed in the mouths of anonymous individuals. This is important, for in these cases the speakers of the pronouncements are less important than the sayings' contents or the people to whom they were addressed. Professor Tannehill drew my attention to the fact that in Tos. Ber. 3:20, M. Ber. 1:3, and Sifra 94a the person to whom the saying is directed is named, even though the person who uttered the pronouncement is anonymous. Sifré Deut. 80 does not seem to me to be similar to anything in the Gospels. Sifra 94a and M. Ber. 1:3 seem to me to be correction stories. Tos. Ber. 3:20 is similar to a commendation story. To my mind the Jewish author of Sifré Num. 131 wants us to take it as a commendation story.

3.4   These twenty-five pericopae from the Tannaitic collections are the closest parallels to Bultmann's *apophthegmata* which I could find. We have seen that some of the Jewish sources closely parallel the accounts in the Gospels, while others do not. We have seen that several of the passages in the Tannaitic sources can be classified according to Tannehill's types, while others do not seem to easily fit into his schema. We have also noted that in the rabbinic texts the pronouncement may be assigned to an anonymous individual or to several people at the same time. Neither of these phenomena are encountered in the Gospels. Thus, the Tannaitic materials show some affinity with the stories in the Gospels as well as evidencing some differences.

4.   Tannaitic Sources and the Individual

4.1   Given the scope of the Tannaitic corpus, twenty-five pericopae is not a significant number. Surely, it is much less than Bultmann's remarks would lead us to expect. Furthermore, some of the Tannaitic examples differ greatly from the Gospel material, for in some of the former the personality of the one who uttered the pronouncement is ignored. In the Gospels, on the other hand, the personality of the one who recited the pronouncements is the central focus. I would suggest that the relatively small number of pronouncement stories present in the Tannaitic corpus and the neglect of the personality of the "pronouncer" in some of the stories are part of a pattern. Tannaitic literature is generally unconcerned with the personality of a single individual or of select groups of individuals. Because the most important reason for the collection and/or creation of pronouncement stories is an interest in the "pronouncer," we can easily explain why we encounter so few pronouncement stories in the Tannaitic stratum. Furthermore, this lack of concern for individual personality can also explain why a pronouncement can be attributed to an anonymous individual or group of individuals, to more than one person at the same time, or to more than one person in succession.

4.2   W. S. Green has recently presented a detailed analysis of the way in which the authors of the rabbinic texts, in general, and the Tannaitic collections, in specific, have submerged the personalities of the individual sages in the vast sea of the collective "rabbis." First, Green notes (79) that rabbinic literature does not contain a single "systematic or coherent" biography of a single sage. We do not find in rabbinic literature any parallels to the Gospels' accounts of Jesus' life or his teaching activity, nor do we find any parallels to Plutarch's *Lives* or to Diogenes Laertius' *Lives and Opinions of Eminent Philosophers*. As Neusner has demonstrated (1971:III, 246–87), what little biographical information we do possess about early rabbinic figures comes from Amoraic, not Tannaitic documents. He notes that the Jews became interested in supplying biographical information about their sages at the same time that the Persians were presenting biographical information about their Magi. Second, Green states that the "features of . . . [rabbinic] documents suggest that their agenda surpass the teachings of any single master" (80). In support of his claim, Green points to the facts that rabbinic literature contains "a substantial amount of unattributed material" and that these "documents a not constructed around the sayings of any individual, but follow either a thematic, formal, topical, or scriptural arrangement in which the teachings or opinions of various masters are gathered to address a single issue or to interpret a particular verse of Scripture" (80).

4.21   To my mind, the most striking feature of the rabbinic texts to which Green draws attention, pointing to the editors' lack of concern for the personalities of the individual sages, is the appearance of a rather small number of literary forms into which the sayings of all the sages are cast /7/. Green writes: "Forms by nature remove us from a historical figure because they 'package' or epitomize his thought, obscure idiosyncracy and unique modes of expression, and thereby conceal distinctive elements of personality, character, and intellect" (81).

4.22   It is incorrect to claim that the creators of the Tannaitic corpus were totally uninterested in the personalities of individuals. The material presented above provides examples of both commendation stories and objection stories; both types center on the actions and personalities of individuals. It is of interest to note that when we do find Tannaitic passages in which the personality of an individual serves as the focus, some of the stories appear as pronouncement stories. This fact seems to support my claim: If the editors of the Tannaitic documents were more interested in the personalities of the sages, they would have transmitted to us more pronouncement stories

4.23   Some may argue that because we probably have only a small amount of the material available to the original editors of our texts it is impossible for us to claim that pronouncement stories did not exist in abundance at the time that the Gospels were being created. Such an argument is flawed. If such stories were available to the editors of our documents, we must explain why they chose not to transmit them to us. We would have to conclude that the reasons which led the editors of the Gospels to include pronouncement stories were not of import for the editors of the Tannaitic texts. This fact would seem to undercut Bultmann's assumption and assertion that the pronouncement story was an important literary unit of rabbinic literature at the time that the Gospels were composed.

4.3   It is this lack of interest of the editors of the Tannaitic documents in the lives and personalities of the Tannaim which makes the enterprises of the Gospels' writers appear to be non-Jewish. The whole concept of writing a Gospel, much less of collecting the pronouncements of great men, is foreign to the mind-set of the Tannaim as we find it expressed in the literature which has been transmitted to us, perhaps with the exception of Mishnah Avot. Bultmann's ideas concerning the relationship between the pronouncement stories in the Gospels and rabbinic literature are incorrect, and they are incorrect because the two bodies of literature were interested in different things. The rabbinic literature was interested in the word of God as revealed at Sinai and transmitted faithfully from Moses to the rabbis. The Christian literature was interested in the word of God as it found expression in the thought and action of Jesus of Nazareth. To the former, the personalities of the transmitters of God's word were unimportant; to the latter, the personality of the transmitter was in itself equal to God's word.

5.   Conclusions

5.1   We have seen that Bultmann's claims are incorrect; the relevant Jewish texts do not provide a large number of good parallels to the selections from the Christian Bible which Bultmann analyzed. Surely, we have many fewer Tannaitic pronouncement stories than Bultmann's remarks would lead us to expect. We have suggested that the reason we have so few Tannaitic pronouncement stories as compared to the Gospels is the different attitudes of the Gospel writers and the editors of the Tannaitic collections. The former were most concerned with Jesus' personality, while the latter were relatively unconcerned with the personalities of the Tannaim.

5.2   Bultmann's assumption that the rabbinic dialogues in general, because of their give-and-take, provide analogies to the pronouncement stories of the Gospels seems to me to be incorrect. First, dialogues are fairly rare in the rabbinic collections (Neusner, 1971:III, Chap. 1). Second, the rabbinic examples are most often concerned with *halakhic* or exegetical matters, and they seldom end with a saying which serves as the focal point of the whole dialogue. Because the dialogues are often between rabbis of equal stature, the final statement often lacks the importance of Jesus' remarks. The following example is fairly typical of the Tannaitic dialogue:

M. *Shebu.* 3:5: R. Ishmael says: "One is liable only [for an oath sworn] about the future, for it is said: *To do evil or to do good*" (Lev. 5:4). R. ʿAqiba said to him: "If so, I [can] only [learn about oaths] which contain matters of good and evil. From where [can I learn about oaths] which do not contain matters of good and evil?" [Ishmael] said to him: "[You can learn about these oaths] from an extension of Scripture." ['Aqiba] said to him: "If Scripture can be extended to include this, Scripture can be extended to include that."

Although the dialogue flows towards the end, it clearly lacks the dynamic of the pronouncement story. It is a discussion between rabbis of equal stature which focuses upon exegetical techniques and a point of *halakhah*. It is not the presentation of the impressive wisdom of a unique individual.

5.3   When we compare the passages from the Tannaitic corpus which are collected here with the examples my colleagues have assembled from the Greek authors, it becomes clear that the Greek sources provide better parallels for the Gospels' pronouncement stories than do the rabbinic sources. Following the line of research presently being taken by my colleague Professor Vernon K. Robbins /8/, I would suggest that the authors of the Gospels were influenced by Greek works on the philosophers and politicians in their use of pronouncement stories. It is likely that this borrowing was done in order to paint the Jewish Jesus in colors familiar to the Greek reader. By placing Jesus' sayings in a literary pattern familiar to the Greek reader, the authors of the Gospels were able to suggest that Jesus' words were as impressive as those of any philosopher, hero, or politician.

NOTES

/1/   Bultmann lists more sources in his notes on pages 42–43. M. A. Z. 4:7 is the only Tannaitic source in these lists.

/2/   Sanders offers the best recent discussion of the biases of the works on which Bultmann relied and of Bultmann himself.

/3/   The following are the only Tannaitic sources in the lists cited in 1.1 and 1.3: M. A. Z. 3:4, M. Ber. 2:5, M. Ber. 2:6, Mekh. Ish. Jethro 6, Tos. Pes. 1:27, M. A. Z. 2:7, and M. Avot 2:6.

/4/   The Amoraic period is roughly the period from the middle of the third century to the end of the seventh century C.E.

/5/   Towner (3–4) also draws attention to the *ma aseh* formula.

/6/   This is the interpretation of the traditional commentators to Sifré.

/7/   Neusner (1971) first drew attention to and analyzed the forms in which the traditions of the Tannaim were cast. Since Neusner's first study a few new forms have been discovered. For example, Porton (1978).

/8/   In a soon to be published monograph Robbins convincingly argues that the structure of the Gospel of Mark closely parallels sections of Xenophon's life of Socrates.

WORKS CONSULTED

a. *Secondary Works*

Bultmann, Rudolf
    1968   *The History of the Synoptic Tradition.* Rev. ed. Translated by John
                    Marsh. New York: Harper and Row.

Green, William S.
    1978   "What's in a Name? The Problematic of Rabbinic 'Biography.'" Pp.
                    77–96 in W. S. Green (ed.), *Approaches to Ancient Judaism: Theory
                    and Practice.* Brown Judaic Studies I. Missoula: Scholars Press.

Goodblatt, David M.
    1979   "The Babylonian Talmud." Pp. 257–336 in W. Haase (ed.), *Aufstieg
                    und Niedergang der römischen Welt,* vol. II. 19.2. Berlin and New
                    York: W. de Gruyter.

Neusner, Jacob
    1970   *Development of a Legend.* Leiden: E. J. Brill.
    1971   *The Rabbinic Traditions about the Pharisees before 70.* Leiden: E. J.
                    Brill.
    1973   *Eliezer Ben Hyrcanus: The Tradition and the Man.* Leiden: E. J.
                    Brill.

Porton, Gary G.
    1976   *The Traditions of Rabbi Ishmael, Part I.* Leiden: E. J. Brill.
    1977   *The Traditions of Rabbi Ishmael, Part II.* Leiden: E. J. Brill.
    1978   "According to Rabbi Y: A Palestinian Amoraic Form." Pp. 173–188 in
                    W. S. Green (ed.), *Approachs to Ancient Judaism: Theory and
                    Practice.* Brown Judaic Studies I. Missoula: Scholars Press.
    1979   *The Traditions of Rabbi Ishmael, Part III.* Leiden: E. J. Brill.
    1981   *The Traditions of Rabbi Ishmael, Part IV.* Leiden: E. J. Brill.

Sanders, Ed Parish
    1977   *Paul and Palestinian Judaism.* Philadelphia: Fortress.

Tannehill, Robert
    forthcoming   "Types and Functions of Apophthegms in the Synoptic Gospels." In H.
                    Temporini and W. Haase (eds.), *Aufstieg und Niedergang der
                    römischen Welt,* vol. II.25.1. Berlin and New York: W. de Gruyter.

Towner, W. Sibley
    1976   Unpublished report submitted to the Pronouncement Story Work
                    Group.

b. *Tannaitic Texts*

Finkelstein, Louis
1969   *Siphrê ad Deuteronomium*. New York: The Jewish Theological
              Seminary.

Horovitz. H. S.
1966   *Siphrê d'be Rab*. Jerusalem: Wahrmann Books.

Horovitz, H. S., and Rabin, I. A.,
1960   *Mechilta d'Rabbi Ishmael*. Jerusalem: Bamberger and Wahrmann.

Lauterbach, J. Z.
1933   *Mekhilta de Rabbi Ishmael*. Philadelphia: Jewish Publication Society
              of America.

Lieberman, Saul
1955   *The Tosefta: Zera'im*. New York: The Jewish Theological Seminary.
1962   *The Tosefta: Mo'ed*. New York: The Jewish Theological Seminary.
1967   *The Tosefta: Nashim*. New York: The Jewish Theological Seminary.

Weiss, Isaac H.
1946   *Torat Cohanim*. New York: Om Publishing Co.

Zuckermandel, M.S.
1963   *Tosefta*. Jerusalem: Wahrmann Books.

VARIETIES OF SYNOPTIC
PRONOUNCEMENT STORIES

Robert C. Tannehill
Methodist Theological School in Ohio

ABSTRACT

This essay applies the typology developed in the introductory essay to synoptic pronouncement stories. Five of the six types are well represented in the synoptic Gospels. Especially noteworthy are a group of hybrid stories combining commendation with correction or objection, an important group of well-developed quest stories, and a group of testing inquiries which show more dramatic tension than the other inquiries. The stories of each type are listed, sometimes with brief explanation. Differences in usage of the types by the three synoptic Gospels are noted. Features of the climactic sayings and preliminary dialogues which are common, though optional, in certain types are also noted. The ways in which the story types function to change the attitudes and commitments of hearers and readers are explained.

0.1   The typology discussed in the essay which introduces this volume provides a useful framework for the study of synoptic pronouncement stories. It highlights the differing relationship between the climactic response in a pronouncement story and the situation which provokes that response, and this relationship provides clues to the functions which these stories are shaped to perform in communication between speaker and hearer or writer and reader. I have discussed these matters in two previous articles. The article on "Types and Functions of Apophthegms in the Synoptic Gospels" (Tannehill, forthcoming) supplements this essay by providing more detailed discussion of individual texts and of my reasons for relating them to particular types. This previous article also discusses the functions of the types of pronouncement stories, a discussion which is carried further in my article on "Attitudinal Shift in Synoptic Pronouncement Stories" (Tannehill, 1980). Some overlap with these previous articles is unavoidable. To reduce this to a minimum, I will simply list the texts which I judge to belong to each type, except in some cases where explanation is needed and can be briefly given. I will discuss certain features of composition, especially of the climactic sayings and the preliminary dialogues, which seem to be characteristic of the various types. Some differences among the three synoptic Gospels in the use of the pronouncement story will also be noted. Finally, I will summarize my understanding of the function of each of the pronouncement story types.

0.2   I do not assume that each of the texts I discuss is a pre-Gospel unit of oral tradition. It is quite possible that the formation of pronouncement stories continued into the late, redactional stages of the Gospel tradition, as is suggested by the occurrence of parallel sayings in divergent settings. No attempt will be made to separate material of early and late origin, beyond noting that certain scenes (especially inquiries), though marked as separate narrative episodes by a change of setting and/or characters, comment on material in a previous scene, indicating that they did not have an independent origin.

0.3   Before dealing with the five types of synoptic pronouncement story, the following general comments can be made: The frequency with which Greek authors of the Roman period use one sentence pronouncement stories, with the occasion for the pronouncement reduced to a subordinate clause (often a participial clause) /1/, makes the rarity of this construction in the synoptic Gospels noteworthy. The Gospels tend to use several sentences in paratactic relation, resulting in a somewhat longer story. Longer stories are not absent from the non-Christian authors /2/, but the lack of use in the Gospels of the common one sentence story is remarkable. Luke is a partial exception. There we do find some tendency to describe the occasion for a pronouncement in a participial clause (see Luke 3:15, 17:20, 21:5).

0.31   It is also characteristic of Luke to place a parable in a pronouncement story setting, where the parable becomes the response to some situation which is briefly described. Luke 7:36–50, 10:25–37, 12:13–21, 15:1–32, 18:9–14, 19:11–27 are examples /3/. There is some overlap here with the tendency, discussed below (see 3.6), to reply to critics by pointing to an analogy for the criticized behavior. This tendency is found in all three synoptic Gospels.

1.   Correction Stories

1.1   The following correction stories are found in Mark: 1:35–38 par. Luke (Jesus departs from Capernaum), 9:33–37 par. Matt, Luke /4/ (who is greatest?), 9:38–40 par. Luke (the strange exorcist), 10:35–45 par. Matt (request of James and John), 11:15–17 par. Matt, Luke (casting out the traders), 12:18–27 par. Matt, Luke (question about the resurrection), 13:1–2 par. Matt, Luke (the great temple buildings). Possibly 8:11–12 (refusal of a sign) and 12:35–37 par. Matt, Luke (David's son) should also be included /5/.
        In addition, Matthew has the following correction stories: 4:1–11 par. Luke (the temptations), 8:19–20 par. Luke (the homeless Son of Man),

8:21–22 par. Luke (let the dead bury the dead), 11:20–24 (woes on Galilean towns), 17:24–27 (the temple tax), 18:21–22 (forgive seven times?). Luke alone has the following correction stories: 3:15–17 (the people suspect that John is the Christ), 9:61–62 (plowing and looking back), 11:27–28 (blessing of Jesus' mother), 12:13–21 (request to divide an inheritance), 13:1–5 (repentance or destruction), 14:7–11 (places at table), 14:12–14 (inviting guests to dinner), 17:20–21 (the kingdom among you), 18:9–14 (the Pharisee and the tax collector), 19:11–27 (the pounds), 19:41–44 (weeping over Jerusalem), 22:24–27 (dispute about greatness at the Last Supper), 23:27–31 (the weeping women). Possibly 9:52–56 (rejection at a Samaritan village) and 13:31–33 (warning against Herod) should also be included.

There are also hybrid pronouncement stories which combine correction with another type of development. The following stories combine correction and commendation: Mark 3:31–35 par. Matt, Luke (Jesus' true family), 10:13–16 par. Matt, Luke (blessing the children), 12:41–44 par. Luke (the poor widow), 14:3–9 par. Matt (the anointing). The following stories combine correction with testing inquiry: Mark 10:2–9 (question about divorce), Matt 12:38–42 (request for a sign), 16:1–4 (second request for a sign).

1.2   The large number of correction stories found only in Luke is noteworthy. While only five correction stories are unique to Matthew (including hybrids), there are 13–15 correction stories which are unique to Luke. This observation should be considered along side the fact that the correction story is the most common type of pronouncement story in a number of non-Christian authors /6/.

1.3   Matt 12:38–42 and 16:1–4, scenes in which Jesus responds to a request for a sign, contain a strong corrective element. A generation that seeks a sign is "evil and adulterous"; the men of Nineveh and the queen of the south will condemn it. Nevertheless, Jesus is also being tested and a response is made to the request: Jesus points to the sign of Jonah. Since Jesus both corrects and responds to a testing request by supplying an answer, these stories are hybrid, combining correction and testing inquiry. Mark 8:11–12, the refusal of a sign, 12:18–27, the question about the resurrection, and Matt 4:1–11, the temptations, are somewhat different. In all these stories Jesus is being tested. This is explicit in Mark 8:11–12 and Matt 4:1–11, and is indicated in Mark 12:18–27 by the fact that the question is based on a premise which the questioners reject. It does not arise from a search for truth but is a trick question designed to embarrass Jesus. However, in these stories Jesus does not answer the question or respond to the requests, except by correcting them. These stories are simply corrections, not hybrids, though the tension in the stories is heightened by the indications that Jesus is being tested.

1.4   In a correction story the responder takes a position that contrasts with and corrects the position assumed through word or action by some other party. It is not surprising, then, that the climactic saying in a correction story often contains a negation and a contrast. In a number of cases the response is formulated by using a negation followed by a strong "but" (*alla* or *plēn*), as in Mark 10:43–45; 12:25, 27; Matt 4:4; 18:22; Luke 23:28. In other cases we find a negation followed directly by the reason for the negative response (often expressed in a *gar* or *hoti* clause), as in Mark 9:39, 10:14, Luke 17:20–21. A corrective response may also be expressed in an antithetical aphorism, a brief saying in which the corrected attitude is paradoxically tied to its opposite, as in Mark 9:35, 10:43–44, Luke 18:14 /7/.

1.41   The usefulness of these speech patterns in corrective responses can help us to recognize correction stories where there might otherwise be some doubt. When a position as to what is right or expedient is clearly expressed in the provoking setting by an action or statement, or is clearly assumed by a question or request, and then is corrected in the response, the corrective movement in the story is clear. However, there are cases in which the position being corrected is only made clear in the response. In Luke 13:1–5 certain people tell Jesus about the Galileans killed by Pilate. They do not express an opinion about this. However, Jesus begins by suggesting, in a question, what they may think about these Galileans. Although this is only a possible opinion, the story is designed to correct it, and Jesus expresses this with the common negation followed by "but." The words of Jesus in Luke 14:12–14 are introduced only by an indication that they were addressed to the host who had invited Jesus to dinner. The words, however, are typical of a corrective response (negation followed by "but"), and, since the practice being corrected is the ordinary one, the author of Luke can assume that the host followed it and is being corrected. Similarly, the negations with which the response in Luke 17:20–21 begins lead us to believe that the Pharisees hold the rejected views, even though this is not clearly expressed in their introductory question.

1.5   Correction stories are little dramatic scenes in which tension is disclosed between the corrector and the person or group corrected. This tension may come as a surprise. Unlike the objection stories, the response is not provoked by criticism of the responder. We do not know how the story is going to develop until the response is made, for the position corrected may appear at first to be harmless or even praiseworthy. But the corrective response challenges the common and accepted, or it takes the bad but tolerable and makes it appear very bad indeed. Thus the correction story opens up distance between a position accepted by some important group, perhaps by almost everyone, and the position of the responder, thereby placing a choice before the hearer or reader. Common practice is often on the side of the initial position, but the story is on the side of the responder's challenge. For the pronouncement story is not value-neutral. The response is placed in climactic position and is often phrased with rhetorical power. The responder's view is being recommended; the story is an invitation to readers to change their attitude and actions in line with the challenge of the responder. This challenge involves an appeal to the will and often to the imagination. Although correction stories contain brief supporting reasons (often introduced by *gar* or *hoti*), a pronouncement story is quite different than an extensive dialogue in which positions are thoroughly discussed. Reasons must strike like lightning; there is no room for lumbering argument. On the other hand, the rhetorical impact of words is important, for strong words can provoke new thought, awaken the imagination, and open new perspectives that can lead to change in values and commitments. The dramatic tension between persons, inherent to a correction story, contributes to this rhetorical impact.

The typology I am using calls attention to this important group of correction stories, a type of story not previously recognized. This should increase awareness of their challenging function. Rather than isolating historical facts or religious ideas from their tensive setting, interpreters of these stories should become aware that they embody a movement from one value stance to another and that the reader is being invited to follow that movement.

2.   Commendation Stories

2.1   Most synoptic commendation stories are hybrid. However, this is not the case with three scenes which are concerned with the privileges and authority of one or more of the disciples: Matt 13:51–52 (treasures new and old), 16:13–20 (the blessing of Peter), Luke 10:17–20 (the return of the seventy). The first of these refers back to the preceding parables and so is not a fully independent scene.

The frequency of hybrid pronouncement stories in the synoptic Gospels is significant. Most of the commendation stories not only commend but also correct or answer an objection. In these stories the commending judgment of Jesus contrasts with the judgment of someone else. The hybrid commendation stories are developed for the sake of this contrast. Thus there is tension in these stories, as well as in the corrections, and both types are designed to move the reader away from one attitude toward the attitude which Jesus represents. Four stories combine correction and commendation. In Mark 10:13–16 par. Matt, Luke (the blessing of the children) Jesus not only commends the children for what they represent but also corrects the disciples. In Mark 14:3–9 par. Matt (the anointing) Jesus both commends the woman and corrects those who have criticized her. Both of these stories contain three characters (individuals or groups), one of whom is judged by the other two. The story begins with a negative judgment, which is corrected by Jesus' positive judgment. In Mark 3:31–35 par. Matt, Luke (Jesus' true family) Jesus commends those sitting around him by calling them his mother and brothers and also corrects the previous application of these terms to his natural family. In this case the correction applies not only to the messengers in 3:32 but also to the narrator in 3:31, both of whom have used mother and brothers in the usual way. The initial use of these terms in their normal meaning emphasizes the sudden shift introduced by Jesus. Instead of the expected consistency of viewpoint, the story juxtaposes two different meanings of the same phrase /8/. Mark 12:41–44 par. Luke (the poor widow) is similar, although the correction is not as emphatic. In commending the widow Jesus contrasts her with all the others who contributed to the temple; she put in "more than all." Previously, however, the narrator told us that "many rich were putting in much," while the widow put in only two *lepta*. This reading of the situation, based on ordinary economic values, is corrected by Jesus.

The relationships among the characters in Luke 10:38–42 (Mary and Martha) are similar to those in the blessing of the children and the anointing, but there are also new developments. Martha and Jesus not only make contrasting judgments about Mary, but Mary and Martha also act in contrasting ways. Furthermore, Martha not only criticizes her sister but also Jesus. When Jesus' behavior provokes an objection, to which he must reply, we have an objection story. Hence, this is a hybrid objection-commendation. The two objection-commendation stories in Matt 21:14–16 (out of the mouth of babes) and Luke 19:37–40 (entry into Jerusalem) are similar to each other. In both cases praise of Jesus causes an objection. Jesus' response to the objection also shows his approval of the initial praise, which is explicitly Christological.

2.2   In Matt 16:13–20 the authority of a particular individual (Peter) is being affirmed. In most cases, however, a commendation story commends not so much the person as the values and attitudes represented by the person. In this way the commended person becomes a model for others. The values of the Jesus movement are represented not only by Jesus but also by those whom he commends. Commendation stories recommend these values to the reader. The hybrid stories make us aware that these values are in competition with others. In these stories Jesus not only affirms but negates. His way of thinking is a challenge to other ways of thinking. The story recommends Jesus' attitude, but it also displays the tension between this and other attitudes, which may have a firm hold on ordinary life. So in these stories also a choice is clarified and change in personal attitudes becomes a possibility.

The tendency in commendation stories to present people as models will be developed further in quest stories. In some commendations conflict with ordinary social values is indicated by the commendation of people who are socially inferior (children, the poor widow). This will be a strong tendency in synoptic quest stories.

3.   Objection Stories

3.1   The following objection stories are found in Mark: 2:15–17 par. Matt, Luke (meal with tax collectors), 2:18–22 par. Matt, Luke (fasting), 2:23–28 par. Matt, Luke (plucking grain on the Sabbath), 3:1–6 par. Matt, Luke (Sabbath healing of withered hand), 3:22–30 par. Matt, Luke (Beelzebul controversy), 6:1–6 par. Matt (the prophet in his home town), 7:1–15 par. Matt (eating with defiled hands), 8:31–33 par. Matt (Peter's rejection of the passion announcement), 9:9–13 par. Matt (the resurrection and Elijah), 10:23–27 par. Matt, Luke (the rich and the Kingdom).

In addition, the following objection stories are found in Matthew and Luke: Matt 3:13–15 (John's objection to baptizing Jesus), Luke 2:41–51 (the boy Jesus in the temple), 11:37–52 (against the Pharisees and lawyers), 13:10–17 (Sabbath healing of a woman), 14:1–6 (Sabbath healing of man with dropsy), 15:1–32 (Jesus is accused of eating with sinners and responds with parables).

Luke 16:14–15 and 20:16–18 are not independent stories. The objections in these passages refer back to the preceding teaching of Jesus. In both cases the brief objection and response is not sufficiently important to turn the larger passage into an objection story. They are dependent objection sequences similar to the dependent inquiry scenes that will be mentioned later (see 5.1). In Matt 19:3–12 (the question about divorce) Jesus responds to a testing inquiry and then to two objections to the position which he has taken. Each of the three responses is roughly equal in importance, which suggests that this story has moved away from the climactic ending typical of a pronouncement story and toward a more diffuse dialogue form.

We should also consider those stories in which an objection sequence is combined with another type of development to form a hybrid story. The following stories combine objection and commendation: Matt 21:14–16 (out of the mouth of babes), Luke 10:38–42 (Mary and Martha), 19:37–40 (entry into Jerusalem). There are also some quest stories in which the climax of the story includes Jesus' response to an objection (Mark 2:1–12 par. Matt, Luke, healing of the paralytic; Luke 7:36–50, the sinful woman in the Pharisee's house; 19:1–10, Zacchaeus) or Jesus' approval of another person's response to an objection (Mark 7:24–30 par. Matt, the gentile woman; Luke 23:39–43, the penitent criminal; perhaps Matt 8:5–13, the centurion).

3.2   Although the other types being used in this essay are different from those used by Bultmann, objection stories correspond fairly closely with Bultmann's controversy dialogues. Nevertheless, there are some differences in the texts judged to be examples of the type. Bultmann included Mark 11:27–33, basing his judgment on a shorter, reconstructed version of the story (Bultmann: 18–19. E. T. 19–20). However, in its present form, this appears to be a testing inquiry. In the first part of his discussion of apophthegms (9–20, 25–26. E. T. 12–21, 26–27), Bultmann correctly distinguished stories based on an objection to something that has already happened from stories which begin with a question by opponents concerning Jesus' position, which is not known. Later, however, he ignores this distinction and includes Mark 12:13–17, 12:18–27, and 10:2–12 in his general discussion of controversy dialogues (50–51. E. T. 48–49). I do not include these passages in the objection stories. On the other hand, I do include a number of passages omitted by Bultmann: Mark 6:1–6 par., 8:31–33 par., 9:9–13 par., 10:23–27 par., Matt 3:13–15, Luke 2:41–51, 11:37–52, 15:1–32, and the hybrid stories Mark 7:24–30 par., Matt 21:14–16, Luke 10:38–42, 19:1–10, 19:37–40, 23:39–43. The difference between Bultmann's interest in the history of the pre-Gospel tradition and my interest in the rhetorical function of the story forms is apparent here as well as in the quite different typologies when we move beyond Bultmann's controversy dialogues.

3.21   Although Bultmann designated Mark 6:1–6 (the prophet in his home town) a biographical apophthegm (30–31. E. T. 31–32), it appears to me to be a good example of an objection story. To be sure, the questions in 6:2–3 are not clearly negative apart from the comment "And they took offense at him." But this statement clearly indicates that the preceding questions constitute an objection of the townspeople to one of their own claiming or exercising such unusual powers. The saying of Jesus in 6:4 is a relevant response. Jesus describes such an objection as the strange exception to the honor which all others are willing to give a prophet. An attitude so out of step with the judgments of others is dubious.

3.22   Martin Dibelius regarded Luke 2:41–51 (the boy Jesus in the temple) as an outstanding example of a legend (Dibelius: 103–106. E. T. 106–109). I do not deny its legendary features, but careful consideration of the central tension of the plot shows that it follows the pattern of an objection story. After an unusually long narrative introduction, Jesus' mother expresses her objection to her son's behavior, using a question beginning with "why," a style common in objection stories. The climactic pronouncement is a response to this objection.

3.3   The order of the story elements in the Sabbath healing stories varies, causing some uncertainty in relating them to the types. In Mark 3:1–6 the opponents do not express an objection. Nevertheless, their negative attitude toward Sabbath healing is indicated in v. 2. Jesus' position on the matter also seems fairly clear. The opponents anticipate what Jesus is going to do, and their negative attitude is an anticipatory objection to the healing that follows. The evangelist also suggests that it is based on past knowledge of Jesus' behavior. The introductory statement "He entered again into the synagogue" recalls to the reader Jesus' previous Sabbath miracle in Mark 1:21–28. Thus the evangelist can view the negative attitude of the opponents as an indication of their objection to a way of acting which has already been demonstrated and which they anticipate will be confirmed. Jesus responds to this objection with both words (3:4) and action (the healing). In Luke 14:1–6 the negative attitude of the opponents is indicated by the statement that they were "watching" or "lying in wait" for him (a reminiscence of the Sabbath healing in Luke 6:6–11) and by the indication in 14:6 that they would have liked to "answer back" but could not. In this story the healing precedes Jesus' principal pronouncement, making clear that his words are a defense of his behavior against the objection implied in the Pharisees' attitude. Matt 12:9–14, although parallel to Mark 3:1–6, has been changed sufficiently to make judgment difficult. This is the first Sabbath healing in Matthew, so we cannot assume that the opponents are acting on the basis of previous knowledge. In contrast to Mark, Jesus is asked a question. This is not an objection but merely asks Jesus to express his opinion about Sabbath healing. Jesus responds to the question with a definite answer before the healing takes place. This suggests that we can understand the story as a testing inquiry, with a healing miracle providing a framework. Nevertheless, the statement that the opponents are asking "in order that they might accuse him" (parallel to Mark) may indicate that they anticipate Jesus' position and implicitly object to it. If so, Jesus responds as expected; the anticipation proves correct and constitutes an objection to a position which Jesus actually holds and which he must defend.

3.4   As with correction stories, there are more uniquely Lukan objection stories than uniquely Matthean. Matthew preserves more of the Markan objection stories and elaborates them, adding arguments to refute the opponents, but has few additional ones.

3.5   In non-Christian authors short objection stories are often introduced by a participle of *oneidizō* /9/. This construction is not used in the Gospels.

3.6   A remarkable aspect of the responses in objection stories is the frequent use of rhetorical questions, often combined with an appeal to an analogous situation /10/. A question, even a rhetorical one, seeks a response. The judgment of the objector is asked for. This judgment is guided by the question, which makes a particular conclusion seem inevitable. The question asks the objector to affirm this conclusion, which requires a change of mind. Although the reactions of other people to Jesus' climactic words are seldom indicated in the pronouncement stories, there is a sense in which these objection stories are deliberately incomplete until these questions are answered. Those who overhear what is being said (including the readers of the Gospels) must give their own answers to Jesus' argumentative question. The rhetorical question brings a decision into focus. It puts the matter into a perspective which contrasts with the perspective from which the objectors are judging and asks all of us to decide from this new perspective. In Mark 3:4 Jesus' question poses a single alternative in light of which the decision should be made. If the alternative is accepted, the required answer is clear. Mark 2:9 is somewhat similar. It is much more common, however, for the question to appeal to an analogous situation where behavior like that of Jesus is generally accepted. We react to situations because we judge them to be like other situations which we understand and evaluate in certain ways. Our reaction can change if we discover a different likeness which suggests a different understanding of the situation and a different judgment of what is right and wrong. In the following passages from objection stories Jesus argues by analogy, asking in a question for a judgment about an analogous situation, a judgment which implies a new way of viewing the matter under debate: Mark 2:19 par., 3:23–26 par., Matt 12:11, 12:27 par., 12:29, Luke 7:41–42, 11:39–40, 13:15–16, 14:5, 15:4–10. In Luke 7:41–42 and 15:4–10 we find parables with questions, suggesting that some of the parables are developed forms of these arguments by analogy. In Mark 2:17 par., 2:21–22 par., 3:27 there are appeals to analogies which are not formulated as questions. The last two texts use statements with *oudeis*, and in Matthew's parallel to Mark 3:27 Mark's "no one can . . ." is transformed into "how can anyone . . . ," showing that the rhetorical questions in objection stories relate closely to implicit statements.

In some cases the argumentative question with which Jesus responds to an objection contains an appeal to Scripture (Mark 2:25–26 par., Matt 12:5, 21:16, Luke 20:17). In the first two cases this also involves argument from analogy. The phrase "have you never read," often used to introduce these appeals to Scripture, contains a reproach for not knowing what should have been known. The question in Luke 2:49 expresses a similar reproach, although it is not an appeal to Scripture.

3.61   In addition to rhetorical questions and analogies, we often find general statements of principle in the responses in objection stories. Thus the story moves from a specific occasion to a disclosure of the basic principle by which actions and attitudes on such occasions should be governed, combining the vividness of a particular encounter with a general disclosure of God's will or the meaning of Jesus' mission. These general statements are often formulated antithetically, emphasizing the contrast between what is being said and another point of view (these are similar to some correction responses) or emphasizing two contrasting possibilities /11/. Mark 2:17 par., 2:27, 7:15 par., Luke 7:47, 16:15 are examples. General statements which are not antithetical are found in Mark 2:10 par., Luke 11:41, 19:10.

3.7   In an objection story tension arises at an earlier point than in a correction story. In corrections it is the corrective response of Jesus that makes clear that something is amiss. This may come as a surprise. In objection stories, however, conflict is initiated by the objector. The peculiar behavior of Jesus and his disciples has been noted in the public domain and has provoked a reaction. Thus correction stories initiate tension, while objection stories are fitted to reflect the tension which already exists because of conflicts between the Jesus movement and its environment. Bultmann's assertion (41. E. T. 40–41) that the controversy dialogues are related to the "apologetic and polemic" of the early church fits many of these stories well. Indeed, a few passages involve sharp counterattacks against the objecting group, suggesting hard lines of division. These are passages in which the response is long and composite, contrasting with the brief and pointed response which is typical of the pronouncement story (see Mark 7:1–15 par., Matt 12:22–37, Luke 11:37–52). However, in most cases Jesus speaks to the issue, rather than attacking the objector, and appeals for agreement in spite of the wide gulf separating the parties to the conversation. In question, analogy, and forceful statement of principle, Jesus presents his perspective, and both the power of the words and their story setting help them to take root in the memory and imagination of the reader, where they may provoke new thought. Although Jesus replies to outsiders in many of these stories, his words are also relevant to his followers. As with other groups, the special concerns and values of the Jesus movement are subject to erosion. The words of Jesus in objection stories often disclose the fundamental concerns behind peculiar practices and seek to reawaken commitment to these fundamentals.

An objection is a challenge to Jesus and his authority. Such situations carry risk for Jesus and those who honor him. The objection stories and the testing inquiries highlight the ability of Jesus to meet such challenges. The powerful wisdom and authority of Jesus stand out as they are put to the test. Thus these stories are also indirect praise of Jesus.

4.   Quest Stories

4.1   Although a few possible examples of quest stories outside the synoptic Gospels have been found /12/, they appear to be rare, while this is an important group of pronouncement stories in the synoptics. Some of these stories concern people who seek for and receive healing for themselves or others. We might suppose that the synoptic quest story developed through a combination of the healing miracle story with the pronouncement story. However, this does not explain a majority of the cases. Only four of the nine stories in the synoptic Gospels concern persons in quest of healing. Furthermore, the inclusion of healing does not necessarily lead to a quest story, for there is a significant group of objection stories which report a healing. Evidently some early Christian story tellers were interested in the figure of the quester, who becomes prominent in these stories.

4.2   Quests are usually longer and more elaborate than most pronouncement stories. They can incorporate features of the other types. In them Jesus may correct and commend, or answer an objection and commend. However, these features are parts of the story of a quest, and it is this quest which provides the central tension of the story and orders the other features as a meaningful development. A quest story discloses the need of a quester and comes to an end by announcing success or failure in meeting that need. This concern with the outcome of the story for the person who encounters Jesus is unusual, for most pronouncement stories end with the pronouncement of the sage, with no indication of how those addressed are affected by this. At most there is indication of a general crowd reaction. But the quest story focuses on the quester. It is his or her need and success or failure which shape the story and are meant to gain our interest. The pronouncement of Jesus relates to this need and has a key role in the success or failure of the quester. Jesus remains the figure of authority in the story and he must certify the success of a quest. The pronouncement which announces the successful quest usually implies the commendation of the quester. Thus, there is a relation between the successful quest (all but one of the synoptic quest stories are successful) and the commendation story, though they differ because the quest emphasizes that a person comes to Jesus with a need and finds the solution to that need. Quests can develop further the tendency in commendation stories to present persons other than Jesus as models to be imitated. Most striking, however, is the strong tendency to present someone with a religious or social liability as a successful quester. Religious inferiors or outcasts receive Jesus' affirmation. The outcome conflicts with the usual expectations of such people. These stories are working against resistance and are seeking to change attitudes, for they present questers with disqualifying characteristics who, in the end, are not disqualified. The negative characteristics of the questers make success doubtful and add to the interest of the stories. These and other blocking factors are often highlighted within the story by being expressed as objections to the quest. The interpreter should pay close attention to such blocking factors, for they often disclose the issue on which the story teller wants to change attitudes.

4.3   Mark 10:17–22 par. Matt, Luke (the rich man) is the only unsuccessful quest story in the synoptic Gospels. Several features of Mark's text encourage a positive reaction to the rich man and sympathy for his quest, resulting in a sense of tragedy when the conflict between riches and the demands of discipleship proves to be too great. Mark 10:28–31 par. Matt, Luke provides an alternative ending to the story of the rich man, for the disciples are pictured as responding positively to the demand made of the rich man (see Tannehill, 1975:149). Mark 12:28–34 (the first commandment) appears to be a quest, although the parallel versions are testing inquiries. Following Jesus' statement of the two love commandments, the scribe makes an unusually long statement (12:32–33). He praises Jesus' answer and emphasizes its importance, which might lead us to compare this story with some inverted commendation stories in which the sage or hero is praised, rather than praising another /13/. However, the scribe introduces something new when he applies Jesus' teaching to the issue of temple sacrifices. The final verse not only commends this as a correct insight but makes a declaration about the religious state of the scribe: "You are not far from the Kingdom of God." Although the personal stake of the scribe in the question which he brings to Jesus is not brought out until the end of the story, this ending appears to move the story beyond commendation to quest. In Matt 8:5–13 par. Luke the centurion also makes a rather long statement, is commended, and receives what he seeks. If 8:7 is a question indicating an initial objection by Jesus (see Bultmann: 39), Matthew's version of this story is quite similar to the story of the gentile woman discussed below. Luke 17:12–19 (the Samaritan leper) moves like other quest stories from an initial indication of a need to an announcement that the need has been fulfilled /14/. In this case this is accompanied by a strong contrast between one leper who shows gratitude and nine lepers who do not. The positive behavior of the one leper is demonstrated before the disclosure of a factor which would be negative for some hearers of this story: the leper is a Samaritan. In vv. 17–18 Jesus criticizes the nine, thereby highlighting the appropriateness of the Samaritan's behavior and making it difficult to deny that Jesus' inclusion of the Samaritan in his saving work is also appropriate.

There is a group of quest stories in which an objection must be overcome for the quest to be successful. If this is the major conflict in the story and if the climax both answers the objection and discloses the outcome of a quest, we may speak of a hybrid objection-quest. This applies to Mark 2:1–12 par. Matt, Luke (the paralytic). It also applies to Mark 7:24–30 par. Matt (the gentile woman). In the latter story Jesus expresses the objection himself and must change his mind. Jesus' final words have a double function: they adopt the woman's reply to the objection as Jesus' own position and announce the success of the quest. In Luke 7:36–50 (the sinful woman in the Pharisee's house) Jesus and the Pharisee take contrasting attitudes to the woman, with the Pharisee objecting to Jesus' behavior and Jesus answering the objection. The woman also represents an attitude toward Jesus which contrasts with that of the Pharisee, as is emphasized in vv. 44–46. Similar contrasting relationships are found in the Mary and Martha story (an objection-commendation), but Luke 7:36–50 is longer and the story is developed as a quest. The woman is introduced as a sinner and at the end Jesus emphasizes to her that her sins are forgiven. Although vv. 48 and 50 may seem like an appendix, they indicate that the story teller understands the story as a quest, which ends appropriately when Jesus certifies to the woman that she has received what she needs. In Luke 19:1–10 the story ends both with the announcement to Zacchaeus of the success of his quest and with Jesus' response to the crowd's objection, as is somewhat awkwardly indicated by the shift in the party addressed in v. 9. Finally, in Luke 23:39–43 (the requests of the crucified criminals) the quester is at center stage, as in other quest stories. His quest is expressed late in the scene (v. 42), but it is to this quest that Jesus responds in his final pronouncement. In responding positively Jesus is also expressing approval of the penitent criminal's response to the first criminal's objection (v. 39), bringing to a resolution both the objection and the quest sequences. Since the objection presupposes the preceding crucifixion narrative, this is not a fully independent story.

4.4   Since quest stories incorporate some of the movements of the other types, they may share some of the same functions. However, quests are unique in the prominent role which they give to the quester. We are presented with the quester's need, and the story continues until we discover whether the quester succeeds or fails in finding the solution to that need. These features help us to experience events from the quester's perspective, and there may be other aspects of the story which encourage hope and sympathy for the quester /15/. In this way readers are encouraged to recognize their own quests in these stories or to become sympathetic to those in need. Tension arises for readers when the need of the quester encourages sympathy and the positive response of Jesus calls for a similar response from the reader, yet an aspect of the quester offends against prejudices. It is striking how many of these stories involve persons who arouse such prejudices: gentiles (Mark 7:24–30, Matt 8:5–13), a sinful woman (Luke 7:36–50) and a sinful cripple (Mark 2:1–12), a Samaritan (Luke 17:12–19), a tax collector (Luke 19:1–10), and a criminal (Luke 23:39–43). These stories function both to invite the outcasts and to create openness for them within the religious community.

The large number of these stories in Luke is noteworthy. Counting stories shared with other Gospels, Luke contains seven of the nine synoptic quest stories. Four of these are unique to Luke.

5.   Inquiry Stories

5.1   There is an important group of testing inquiries in the synoptic Gospels. Apart from these, however, the inquiry stories in the synoptic Gospels are not a large and well-developed group. The dramatic tension which characterizes other types is reduced. In some stories the connection between the question or request and the response is not clear, and some stories, although they are marked as separate scenes through the introduction of a new character and sometimes a new setting, are dependent on previous material, providing clarification of it. Thus we find the following dependent inquiry scenes in which Jesus responds with additional explanation: Mark 4:10–20 par. Matt, Luke; 7:17–23 par. Matt; 9:28–29 par. Matt; 10:10–12; Matt 13:36–43; Luke 12:41–48. In Mark 11:20–25 the withering of the fig tree provokes an exclamation from Peter which seems to function as an inquiry into how this could happen, since Jesus seems to be replying to such a question. This is Matthew's understanding of the scene, for in Matt 21:20 the exclamation becomes a question. Apart from the testing inquiries, the rest of the inquiry scenes are Lukan: Luke 3:10–14 (John's instructions to social groups), 11:1–4 (the Lord's prayer), 13:22–30 (enter through the narrow gate), 17:5–6 (faith). In the last three scenes the words of Jesus have a parallel in another Gospel, but Luke's pronouncement story setting is unique.

5.11   In the inquiry scenes listed above the focus of attention is on the teaching in the responses, and the function of the stories is to convey this teaching. The questions or requests which introduce the responses add little, except that they link the dependent inquiry scenes to preceding material, indicate the general topic of the teaching which follows, and sometimes suggest a particular application of the teaching. Luke 11:1, for instance, suggests that the Lord's prayer is an appropriate answer to a request for a basic pattern of prayer for Jesus' disciples.

5.2   Unlike the other inquiries, the testing inquiries comprise a group of fairly long, dramatically developed stories which are fully capable of independent existence. In a testing inquiry the question or request usually comes from a hostile or skeptical party. It is designed to put the responder to the test. The responder is placed in a critical situation. There is a sense of risk, for the reputation, influence, and perhaps the safety of the responder are at stake. In the synoptic Gospels this situation may be indicated simply by a participial phrase ("testing him"), indicating the inquirer's intention. However, a testing situation also arises when the question or request concerns the status and authority of Jesus. Jesus may respond to a testing question or request by correcting it. Such stories belong with the corrections (see 1.3 above). On the other hand, if the question or request is accepted and answered, we have a testing inquiry. Although the responder is also placed in a critical situation when faced with an objection from a hostile party, the testing inquiry differs from the objection story in that the provoking element is not an objection to something already said or done.

5.21   The following stories are testing inquiries: Mark 10:2–9 par. Matt (divorce), 11:27–33 par. Matt, Luke (Jesus' authority), 12:13–17 par. Matt, Luke (taxes to Caesar), Matt 11:2–6 par. Luke (John's question to Jesus), 12:38–42 (first request for a sign), 16:1–4 (second request for a sign), 22:34–40 (the great commandment), Luke 10:25–37 (loving one's neighbor) /16/. Of the stories in this list, Mark 10:2–9 is a hybrid, for vv. 5–9 both answer the initial question and correct the Mosaic permission /17/. Matt 12:38–42 and 16:1–4 are also hybrids which combine testing inquiry with correction (see 1.3 above). In addition, Mark 8:27–30 par. Luke (Peter's confession) is an inverted testing inquiry, i.e., a testing inquiry in which the person featured in the writing (Jesus) does not respond to the test but poses the testing question /18/. Mark 12:35–37 par. Matt, Luke (David's son) may also be an inverted testing inquiry. If Jesus is denying that the Christ is David's son, the story is a correction; if not, Jesus is posing a testing question. The question concerns the views of a group generally presented as hostile /19/, and they will lose influence if they have no explanation. In this case, no answer is given. The special interest of the author in the requests for a sign gives Matthew's Gospel a slight edge in the number of testing inquiries.

5.22   The repeated use of preliminary counterquestions in synoptic testing inquiries is noteworthy. These questions differ from the rhetorical questions which frequently appear in objection stories (see 3.6 above), and sometimes elsewhere. In objection stories the question is the response or an important part of it; in it Jesus is disclosing his view of the matter. In the testing inquiries Jesus' question is preliminary; it is designed to elicit an answer that will contribute to Jesus' final answer. Therefore, the inquirer's answer (or non-answer) to Jesus' question is recorded as part of the story. We find such questions in Mark 10:3; 11:29–30 par.; 12:16 par.; Luke 10:26, 36. Note also these preliminary questions in the inverted stories: Matt 22:42, Mark 8:27 par. /20/. Through these questions Jesus seizes the initiative in the testing situation. Furthermore, in this way a crucial factor can be brought into the open, where it can be assessed (Mark 10:3), and the inquirers can be made to participate in answering their own questions (Mark 12:16 par.; Luke 10:26, 36), which will make the final answers more difficult to reject.

5.23   There is a significant increase in the dramatic tension in testing inquiries, compared to ordinary inquiry stories, because we are presented with a situation of risk. This tension is often developed through lengthening the story and including several exchanges of dialogue. In these stories there is interest not only in the answer to the inquiry but also in the outcome for the answerer. The responder as a person has something to gain or lose. This can emphasize the response, for an impressive response is all the more impressive when made in a situation of risk. But the testing inquiries also say something about Jesus: his claim to wisdom and authority can pass the test even of difficult questions from hostile questioners. Furthermore, in a number of cases a Christological interest appears in the issues raised, for the questions concern Jesus' authority and status (Mark 8:27–30 par., 11:27–33 par., Matt 11:2–6 par., 12:38–42, 16:1–4; see also Mark 12:35–37 par.).

6.   Description Stories

6.1   Description stories are either very rare or completely lacking in the synoptic Gospels. The only possibility that I have noted is Luke 14:15–24, in which the parable of the great banquet is presented as a response to the statement "Blessed is the one who will eat bread in the Kingdom of God." The parable neither corrects nor commends this statement but reveals a concealed incongruity, for an unexpected group receives this blessing. This is somewhat like the descriptions, but I do not regard it as a clear and convincing example.

7.   Conclusion

7.1   We have a rich group of pronouncement stories in the synoptic Gospels, especially in Mark and Luke, particularly when we consider that the Gospels are connected narratives composed of material of various genres, not just pronouncement story collections. Furthermore, the dramatic possibilities of the pronouncement story are developed. Relevant aspects of the situation are brought out, and persons other than Jesus frequently speak in direct discourse, sometimes more than once. The narrative setting does more than provide a location for a sage's word of wisdom. It helps to present Jesus' words in their significance for those who encounter Jesus, with their challenge to the surrounding world, and in situations that are critical for Jesus himself.

7.2   The typology employed in this essay helps us to do justice to the fact that a pronouncement story is a story with narrative tension and movement, not just a saying with a narrative setting which can be ignored. It helps us to determine the specific ways in which tension appears in these stories. When we consider the particular issues presented in these patterns of tension in individual stories, we can see these stories as narrations of value conflicts, investigate the relation of the story to value conflicts in the historical situation of the early church, and draw conclusions about the way that these stories were meant to influence the value orientation of their readers.

NOTES

/1/   See Diogenes Laertius, *Lives and Opinions of Eminent Philosophers* VI.4 (five pronouncement stories in the first five Greek sentences), VI.5 (two pronouncement stories in the first two Greek sentences; a third in the last sentence).

/2/   They seem to be especially common in Plutarch (and works attributed to him).

/3/   See also Luke 14:15-24, where the relation of the parable to the introductory statement by the dinner companion is not very clear.

/4/   In Matthew's version Jesus' response introduces a long discourse. Also, Matt 18:1-5 lacks Mark's reference to the disciples arguing about greatness, weakening the correction. Nevertheless, the phrase "unless you turn and become . . ." seems to imply correction.

/5/   Mark 12:35-37 par. is a correction if Jesus is rejecting the view that the Christ is David's son.

/6/   The correction story is the most common type of pronouncement story in Diogenes Laertius' *Lives* (see sect. 4 in the article by Poulos in this volume), Lucian's *Demonax*, Philostratus' *Life of Apollonius of Tyana*, and (pseudo?)-Plutarch's *Sayings of Kings and Commanders*, among other works.

/7/   On antithetical aphorisms see Tannehill (1975:88–107).

/8/   On Mark 3:31–35 see further Tannehill (1975:165–71).

/9/   See Diogenes Laertius, *Lives and Opinions of Eminent Philosophers* VI. 4, 6, 56, 58, 66, 67, etc.

/10/   This was noted by Bultmann (42. E.T. 41).

/11/   Compare my discussion of the antithetical aphorism in Tannehill (1975:88–101).

/12/   In the articles in this volume, see Alsup sect. 6; Poulos sect. 2; Tannehill, "Introduction" 2.4. See also Philostratus, *Life of Apollonius of Tyana* I. ix.

/13/   See Robbins' discussion of laudations in his essay in this volume.

/14/   In the context of this story, "Your faith has saved you" refers to a salvation which includes but goes beyond healing. The strong contrast with the nine in vv. 17–18 suggests that this statement applies to the Samaritan leper in a way that it does not apply to the other nine healed lepers.

/15/   Such encouragement is especially clear in the story where the quester fails. Mark 10:17, 19–21 emphasize the rich man's reverential attitude, religious commitment, and Jesus' positive response.

/16/   It is possible that Matt 12:9–14 should also be included. See 3.3 above.

/17/   In Matthew's version, however, Jesus' answer to the testing inquiry is followed by two objections.

/18/   Matthew transforms this into a commendation story by the addition of Matt 16:17–19.

/19/   However, in Luke the source of the opinion is unclear.

/20/   The function of the question in Mark 8:27 par. is somewhat different. It elicits a preliminary answer which contrasts with the final one.

WORKS CONSULTED

Bultmann, Rudolf
1958   *Die Geschichte der synoptischen Tradition.* 4. Aufl. Göttingen: Vandenhoeck & Ruprecht. English trans., *The History of the Synoptic Tradition.* Rev. ed. New York: Harper & Row, 1968.

Dibelius, Martin
1961   *Die Formgeschichte des Evangeliums.* 4. Aufl. Tübingen: Mohr. English trans., *From Tradition to Gospel.* New York: Scribner's.

Tannehill, Robert C.

1975   *The Sword of His Mouth: Forceful and Imaginative Language in Synoptic Sayings*. Philadelphia: Fortress & Missoula: Scholars.

1980   "Attitudinal Shift in Synoptic Pronouncement Stories." Pp. 183–97 in Richard A. Spencer (ed.), *Orientation by Disorientation: Studies in Literary Criticism and Biblical Literary Criticism in Honor of William A. Beardslee*. Pittsburgh: Pickwick.

forthcoming   "Types and Functions of Apophthegms in the Synoptic Gospels." In *Aufstieg und Niedergang der römischen Welt*, ed. Hildegard Temporini & Wolfgang Haase, Band II. 25. 1. Berlin: de Gruyter.

PRONOUNCEMENT STORIES IN THE GOSPEL OF THOMAS

Pheme Perkins
Boston College

ABSTRACT

Examination of pronouncement stories in the Gospel of Thomas (GTh) suggests that while the sayings tradition behind GTh may have preserved other non-
canonical pronouncement story traditions, the Gnostic users of such materials no
longer appreciated the unique dynamics of the genre. Instead, they retained pronouncement story materials when the elements of dialogue permitted assimilation to
the types of dialogue that are characteristic of Gnostic religious discourses. GTh stands
in a tradition of Gnostic writings which associate the revelation dialogue with the
interpretation of Jesus' sayings. That context cannot appreciate the dynamic interaction of the synoptic pronouncement story, since it lacks the imaginative realism of
the synoptic tradition. Such stories can only be seen as esoteric riddles within the
"otherworldly" imagination of Gnosticism.

0.   Since Gnostic literature does not contain either biographical or
realistic narrative, one is hardly surprised to find that pronouncement stories
do not flourish there. Amos Wilder rightly points out that Gnosis fosters a
different religious imagination from the realism characteristic of the Christian gospel. The Gnostic impluse dramatizes Jesus as oracle encountering
human ignorance (Wilder: 38–49). Beardslee's study of proverbs in GTh
reaches similar conclusions. GTh is not interested in the proverb as such. Its
interiorizing exegesis reduces the power of proverbial language as comment
on interpersonal relationships. GTh preserves proverbial sayings of Jesus only
because they are sacred traditions. One suspects that those proverbs in GTh
which do not have synoptic parallels belonged to the tradition of Jesus' sayings prior to its development in Gnostic sayings exegesis /1/. Beardslee lists
several characteristics of GTh traditions which suggest that the author no
longer appreciates the power of the proverbial statement. Paradox and
hyperbole are reduced. Some proverbs have been clarified with additional
comments. Since GTh lacks the biographical context of Jesus' ministry, the
elements of controversy and debate in which these proverbs first appear are

gone. Instead one finds declarative statements. The revealer is, after all, addressing the initiate (Beardslee: 102f.).

0.1   Figure 1 surveys those items in GTh which might be understood as pronouncement stories. We will speak of them as *logia* simply to facilitate reference to the various sections in the conventional numbering. As can be seen from the first column, some have been taken from synoptic pronouncement stories; others are based on isolated sayings or dialogue in the gospel tradition; and a few have no clear parallels in the canonical gospel traditions. Two types of analysis can be applied to these stories. One is to classify them according to the new typology suggested by the work group's study of the pronouncement story. The column "Tannehill" is my attempt at such a classification. There is disagreement over some of the sayings—unavoidably, given the necessity to supply elements of Gnostic context in order to understand them. The second approach to the problem is to see the stories as a function of their sayings and to classify them in accord with the form of saying involved. The column labeled Koester represents the author's attempt to apply Koester's suggestions to this group of logia. The final column indicates some of the typical changes that can be observed in these stories. Some represent a simple introductory question which has been added to sayings or parables from the Jesus tradition. Others have been expanded in the direction of dialogue in line with the use to which such material was put in Gnostic circles. Still others simplify the introduction by having disciples rather than opponents of Jesus ask the question which leads to the saying in question. The simplification of the introductory narrative often deprives these stories of the elements of controversy that they originally involved. It also leaves the individual sayings open for a variety of Gnostic interpretations as the variety in the various commentaries on these sayings shows.

Fig. 1 Pronouncement Stories in GTh

Log.	Syn. Par.	Tannehill	Koester	Changes Introduced
6°	logia	inq.	apoc.	introduction added to sayings
12	(pron.st.)	inq.	rule?	introduction added
13	(pron.st.)	cor. & com.	I AM	expanded into dialogue
18	–	cor.	apoc.beat.	simple introduction
20	parable	inq.	parable	request introduces parable
22	(logia)	com. & cor.	parable/apoc.	expanded into dialogue
24	logia; Johan. dialogue	cor.	proverb	question as introduction
37	–	inq.	parable secondary	question as introduction
43	(logia)	obj.(inq.?)	negative I AM judgment	

Log.	Syn Par.	Tannehill	Koester	Changes Introduced
51	pron.st. (logia)	cor.	apoc.	simple introduction
52	–	cor.	analogy/prophetic	statement introduction
53	–	inq.	negative rule introduction	
60	–	inq.	(dialogue)	tending toward dialogue
61	(logia)	inq. & cor.	I AM	tending toward dialogue
72	pron.st./ parable	cor.	negative I AM	parable omitted
79°	pron.st.	cor.	prophetic/apoc.	
91	logion	cor./testing inq.	apoc.	
99	pron.st	cor.	pron.st.	statement by disciples, not people
100	pron.st. (test)	inq.	rule	opponents omitted
104	test	cor.	rule	vague "they"; motivation for demand is also vague
113	pron.st.	cor.	prophetic/apoc.	disciples ask, not Pharisees
114	–	cor.	rule	

°proverb of beatitude type (Beardslee: 93)
(   ) parallels are not close
com. commendation
cor. correction
inq. inquiry
obj. objection
apoc. apocalyptic saying
pron.st. pronouncement story
Tannehill/Koester author's attempts to classify logia in the categories of Tannehill and Koester.

0.11   The shortening of the narrative setting is only one of the difficulties encountered when one attempts to spell out the formal characteristics of the Gnostic pronouncement stories. Often one cannot state the relationship between the question asked and the response with any precision. The interpretation of a passage may vary considerably depending upon whether one takes it to be a simple inquiry or a correction. In the synoptic tradition the larger context of the gospels establishes distinctions like friend, dull disciple, curious heckler, foe, which help determine the thrust of the pronouncement stories that are included. Here that narrative aid is lacking. Furthermore, Gnostics thrive on such ambiguity. A lack of "fit" between question and answer typifies the larger category of Gnostic dialogue (Rudolph: 80–90; Perkins, 1980:19–28). Modern interpreters of Gnostic sayings material face another problem. Were Gnostics aware of the synoptic context of sayings and parables that have parallels there? If so, some of the dynamics of those stories may have been presupposed by the Gnostic interpreter. If not, one might well

conclude that the sayings which are introduced by brief questions are in
the same category as sayings introduced by "Jesus said" (Fitzmyer: 359).

0.12   It is sometimes possible to resolve the vagueness of the individual
story by creating a somewhat fuller narrative based on other Gnostic evidence. For example, if the disciples are taken to represent church authorities
opposed to the Gnostics—a role often given to Peter (Perkins, 1974:1f.;
Pagels, 1979:27–51)—then Jesus' answers to their questions might be taken
as correction rather than as inquiry. Or, if "the disciples" represent the un-
comprehending mass of orthodox Christians rather than Gnostic believers,
then certain questions might be testing inquiries /2/. The other Gnostic
writings from the same area, Dialogue of the Savior (DialSav) and Thomas
the Contender (ThCont), suggest that esoteric interpretation of the sayings
of Jesus had become an area of controversy between Gnostic and orthodox
Christians (Perkins, 1980:99–112). They contain material parallel to what we
find in some GTh pronouncement stories. Yet there are no longer any pronouncement stories in their traditions of sayings exegesis (Koester/Pagels:
64–69). Thus, they indicate that the pronouncement story passed out of use
in this tradition.

1.   We will not be able to avoid the hermeneutical problems posed by
the pronouncement stories in GTh /3/. They require a larger context in
order to be seen as examples of a specific type, and are part of a tradition
that will soon drop the genre. Yet the type is still preserved in some of the
GTh traditions. We will be able to use parallel material in the other Thomas
traditions to show how such exchanges would have been viewed by the
Gnostic exegetes of that tradition.

1.1   Log. 20 represents a simple transformation of the Mustard Seed
parable into a pronouncement story by addition of an introductory question
(Ménard: 109). It is followed by two rather diffuse passages, logia 21, clearly
not a pronouncement story as it stands, and 22. Tannehill has suggested that
log. 21 might have been an inquiry which ended with Jesus' response about
the children at "give it back to them." However, we would suggest that
perhaps the whole section is based on a Gnostic collection of short parables
such as we find referred to in Apocryphon of James (CG I 8, 5–10; see
Perkins, 1980:149). The collection would have been Mustard Seed (Mark
4:30–32); Children in the Field (variant of Children in the Market, Luke
7:31–35); Householder and the Thief (Matt 24:42–44); Reaper (John 4:35–
38); Children Being Suckled (Matt 21:16?). The whole has been cast as an
instructional dialogue on Gnostic entry into the Kingdom. The question
"What are your disciples like?" that introduces log. 21 is finally answered by
the Gnostic sayings at the end of log. 22 which give the esoteric interpretation of the parables and sayings in the collection.

1.2   Log. 24 has been given a Johannine introduction on the basis of the reference to light in the saying (Ménard: 116) /4/. The other dialogues in the Thomas tradition have expanded on sayings material preserved here. ThCont contains a short dialogue on Jesus as the light which draws the Gnostic ascetic out of the darkness and bestiality of this material world (CG II 139, 12–31; NHLE: 189f.). The conclusion to log. 24 appears in the sayings exegesis of DialSav (CG III 125,18–126,1; NHLE: 231). Later this saying is used to describe the plight of the Gnostic who must remain in the body (126,17–128,6; NHLE: 231f.). Thus, the Thomas tradition consistently used sayings such as this to support an ascetic Christianity. The sayings about the inner Kingdom in GTh were probably interpreted along the same lines. The following exchange in DialSav assures the Gnostic that though no one still in the body can attain/see the place of salvation, Gnostic self-knowledge provides the required insight into the truth of salvation:

> Matthew said, "Lord, I wish [to see] that place of life, [that place] in which there is no evil, but rather, it is [the] pure light."
> The Lord said, "Brother Matthew, you (sg.) cannot see it, as long as you wear the flesh."
> Matthew said, "O Lord, even if [I can] not see it, let me [know it]."
> The Lord said, "Every one [of you] who has known himself has seen it; everything that is fitting for him to do, [he does] it. And he has been [doing] it in his goodness."
>
> (CG III 132, 6–19; NHLE: 233)

This whole section of GTh may have been derived from the tradition of sayings interpretation that has been used to form the end of DialSav. Sayings of Jesus are interpreted in dialogue format to teach Gnostic eschatology (Koester/Pagels: 67f.).

1.3   Other passages in GTh are related to pronouncement stories but seem to have become short instances of Gnostic dialogue. Log. 60 is particularly interesting since it is without synoptic parallel. Jesus asks a question to teach the disciples an allegorical lesson necessary for the ascetic: salvation only comes to those who reject the world before it devours them (Ménard: 161; cp. GPhil 93). It presupposes that the hearer will recognize the oddity of a Samaritan carrying a lamb to Judea. Gnostic exegetical traditions clarify the allegory. Samaritans were considered "types" of soul caught in worldliness but rescued by the Savior's call. Jerusalem represented the psychic place in which "Jews," that is, orthodox Christians, worshiped the creator (Pagels, 1973:86–90). This allegory shows that the exchange in log. 60 may have had a polemic context, the debate between the Gnostic ascetics and orthodox Christians.

2.   Six pronouncement stories in GTh have synoptic parallels. Attempts to find more primitive versions of the synoptic stories in these logia

have not been persuasive. Instead they seem to have been abbreviated by Gnostic exegetes who are no longer interested in particular elements of the stories.

2.1   Log. 72//Luke 12:13f. One of two (log. 79) questions from a non-disciple, this logion opens with "a man asked." Claims that the phrase is more primitive than Luke's "one of the crowd" seem unlikely in view of the fact that log. 79, the other non-disciple logion, refers to someone from the crowd. GTh has probably shifted to "a man." Koester finds the lack of "judge" here more primitive, since he thinks that it was added when Q combined sayings and Son of Man traditions (Koester, 1971b:171). However, Gnostics could well have dropped it from the Q form, since they have no interest in Jesus as judge (Ménard: 173).

2.11   The synoptic parallel is a correction. GTh has expanded the story with a negative I AM saying. I AM sayings in GTh characteristically focus on the confession that Jesus is the revealer (Koester, 1971b:178; and see the end of log. 61). GTh has "corrected" the synoptic story to make it emphasize Jesus' status as transcendent revealer.

2.2   Log. 79//Luke 11:27f.; 23:29. Though it is sometimes claimed that this logion represents the more primitive form of a saying which Luke divided, it seems more likely that GTh brought the two passages together by catch-word. Its ascetic concern with the Gnostic rejection of material and family ties overrides the prophetic and apocalyptic origins of the second saying (Ménard: 180f.).

2.21   Log. 79 belongs to a collection of sayings which may be considered community rules. The disciple is instructed to divorce himself from the religious behavior of Judaism (the orthodox Christians?) and the concerns of the world (Koester, 1971b:184). Log. 53 states such a rule in the form of a question and answer. It may have been derived from a primitive tradition rejecting circumcision (Ménard: 156).

2.3   Log. 99//Luke 8:19–21 also concerns family relations. GTh has shortened synoptic materials (Schrage: 185–189; Ménard: 199). The addition of the promise of entry into the Kingdom stresses the need for Gnostic ascetics to reject all family ties (Ménard: 200; Lincoln: 71f.).

2.4   Log. 100//Mark 12:14–17. Another Gnostic community rule has been created by abbreviating synoptic material. The elements of test and controversy have been dropped from the question about paying taxes. Addition of "me what is mine" focuses attention on the final saying (Ménard: 200; Schrage: 189–192). The conflation of the question about paying taxes to Caesar with that about the temple tax probably antedates GTh, since neither is an issue in the Thomas tradition. Not paying taxes now represents the Gnostic's detachment from material things.

2.5   Log. 104//Mark 2:18–20. Log. 104 has been heavily allegorized so that it no longer resembles its synoptic source (Schrage: 194; Ménard: 204). Log. 6, which has combined several sayings to answer a question about fasting (Schrage: 34–37), probably represents the type of sayings exegesis that underlies this passage. The synoptic parallel vindicated fasting in the early church. Since neither Jesus nor the enlightened soul leaves the bridal chamber, the Gnostic rejects fasting permanently. The additional rhetorical question at the beginning, "What sins have I committed . . . ?", contributes to the Gnostic intrepretation. The sinless Jesus of Gnostic Christology never comes under the dominion of the powers or of their religious practices. Gnostics may have used such sayings to distinguish themselves from orthodox Christians. We might argue that the polemic force of the pronouncement story is exploited in allegorical passages like this one and the exchange in log. 60 about the Samaritan carrying a lamb to Jerusalem. Perhaps log. 104 is a deliberate reformulation of a synoptic story being used by the orthodox to defend their practice of fasting.

2.6   Log. 113//Luke 17:20f. Since the Pharisees no longer pose the question, the story might be read as a simple inquiry rather than as testing inquiry or correction. Gnostics typically claimed that the Kingdom was present (cp. 21, 51, 60; Ménard: 209). This story does not focus on the inwardness of the Kingdom. It merely informs the disciples that the Kingdom is present though invisible to most people (Schrage: 199f.).

2.7   These stories all show signs of Gnostic reformulation of synoptic traditions. Most tend in the direction of dialogue, since the Gnostic is compelled to provide esoteric interpretation of the sayings tradition in order to ground his eschatology and ascetic practice. Within the polemic context of the Thomas tradition, some of these stories might have had overtones of controversy. But those overtones can only be caught by one who presupposes a somewhat larger context of Gnostic exegesis than that presented by GTh itself.

3.   Other pronouncement stories show GTh using synoptic sayings material in similar fashion. In some cases, the divergences between the GTh version and synoptic versions are so great that one must assume independent versions of the sayings had been circulated in the area from which GTh originated. Frequently sayings material has been lifted from synoptic contexts without preserving any of the introductory material. There is no instance in which GTh can be shown to have preserved a more primitive saying that the synoptic tradition has turned into a pronouncement story by addition of introductory material.

3.1   Log. 3 seems to have been derived from Luke 17:20f. Since Luke 17:20f. appears explicitly as part of the exchange in log. 113 (see 2.6), we assume that it also served as the basis for this saying. Other GTh sayings also seem to have been derived from synoptic material through removal of the narrative setting. Log. 31 stems from that about a prophet without honor (Schrage: 75–77; Ménard: 127). Log. 34 uses a saying that does appear independently (Luke 6:39), but in log. 34 it appears in a form closer to the second logion of Matt 15: 12–14 (Ménard: 133; Schrage: 85–88). Perhaps the Thomas tradition had an independent version of this tradition, since log. 40 contains an echo of the first saying in the Matthew passage (Schrage: 95). A similar combination appears in log. 48 and 106. Log. 48 reflects a variety of traditions that have been conflated with Matt 17:20, while log. 106 seems to represent a Gnostic interpretation of the saying in log. 48 (Schrage: 116ff.; cp. the earlier interpretation of a collection of parables in terms of "two made one" in log. 20–22, above 1.1). These examples suggest that GTh did not derive its sayings directly from synoptic pronouncement stories but from a tradition of sayings of Jesus in which they had already been reformulated.

3.2   Three remaining examples of sayings without context are much closer to the synoptic versions. They may have been taken directly from synoptic pronouncement stories. Log. 73 reports Jesus' comment about the crowd prior to the missionary discourse (Matt 9:37f.; Ménard: 172; Schrage: 153–155). Log. 86 preserves the conclusion of the story about offering to follow Jesus (Matt 8:20//Luke 9:58; Ménard: 188; Schrage: 168ff.). The rejection of ceremonial purification in log. 89 follows the pattern of other Gnostic sayings on the same topic (cp. Matt 23:25//Luke 11:39f.; Ménard: 191; Schrage: 170ff.). All of these sayings may have formed a compendium on Gnostic discipleship. Though not presented as pronouncement stories in GTh, the concerns they represent are also reflected in GTh pronouncement stories.

4.   The remaining examples from GTh show similar characteristics. Their sayings represent I AM sayings, prophetic/apocalyptic sayings, and community rules. Some may have been derived from non-Gnostic extra-canonical pronouncement stories. Others seem to be allegorical abridgments of dialogue traditions of Gnostic sayings exegesis.

4.1   Log. 51 seems to be an apocalyptic/prophetic saying that has been taken up into the tradition of Gnostic eschatology (Ménard: 153f.). A non-Gnostic version might have had outsiders as interrogators. The initial question about the coming of the "new age (world)" might have been expanded when the saying was attached to the previous logion in which Jesus instructs the disciples about the answers to be given the powers when the soul ascends to its *anapausis* (see the discussion of the connection between such catechesis and sayings exegesis in the James material; Perkins, 1980:147–148).

4.2   A remark by the disciples about the prophets in Israel provokes a rejection of their authority in log. 52. This brief exchange may reflect a larger debate between Gnostics and their opponents over prophecy. The topic is discussed explicitly in ApocryJas (CG I 6,21–7,10; NHLE: 32). The disciples ask what they are to say to those who ask them to prophesy and are told that prophecy ended with John the Baptist and parables with the earthly life of Jesus (see Perkins, 1980:151f.).

4.3   Log. 18 preserves a beatitude that has been reformulated in light of Gnostic exegesis of John (probably of John 14:5–7; Ménard: 106). *Arche*, often interpreted as the heavenly *anthropos*, represents the place to which the Gnostics return (Pagels, 1973:21–35).

4.4   Log. 22, which we have already discussed as a dialogue reinterpretation of a collection of parables (1.1), concludes with sayings which derive from an independent tradition. "When the two shall be one, the outside as the inside, and the male with the female" is quoted in II Clement 12, and similar words are found in Clement of Alexandria, *Strom.* III 13.92, where they are attributed to the Gospel of the Egyptians. Another Gnostic version appears along with elaborate exegesis in GPhil (CG II 67, 30–68, 26; NHLE: 140f.). There Gnostic eschatology is presented as restoring the unity that existed before Eve was taken out of Adam. Several sayings of Jesus are used to show that Jesus taught this discovery of the true self. Several sayings probably circulated in a group to make up this tradition. Log. 37 seems to be part of the same tradition. It refers to trampling one's garments. The variant of the tradition in Clement of Alexandria has "trampling the garments of shame" (the body) combined with the saying about making the two one /5/. Log. 37 makes it the condition for the vision of Jesus as he truly is (see 1.2).

4.5   Log. 43 provides yet another example of a pronouncement story directed against orthodox Christians. It has been cast as a judgment saying against those who will not accept Jesus as Gnostic revealer, using the I AM format from John 8:28, 58. Jews now represent orthodox opponents. However, the Gnostics may not have created this story. A more primitive tradition could be reflected here in which scribes or Pharisees appeared as interrogators in a testing inquiry. The story would then have concluded with a saying formulated as a paradoxical proverb: "You are like men who love the tree and hate its fruit; or love the fruit and hate the tree." The allegorization and reformulation of the saying have destroyed the dynamic unity of the original.

4.6   Other pronouncement stories represent the conflict over authority between Gnostics and their opponents. Log. 13, a short dialogue rather than a pronouncement story, reformulates the confession of Peter so that Thomas is exalted over the representatives of the orthodox tradition, Matthew and Peter (Perkins, 1974:1f.). The incident has been expanded with a community rule against indiscriminate communication of gnosis. Thomas refuses to divulge what the savior had told him. Individual revelation, which is deliberately not shared with the "twelve," appears in other Gnostic dialogues (GMary BG 10,1–6; NHLE: 472; ApocryJas CG I 2, 29–35; NHLE: 30). Community rules against communicating gnosis to outsiders may underlie this topos, which is used in some revelation dialogues to explain why gnosis is not part of accepted apostolic tradition (see Perkins, 1980:191–201).

4.61   Log. 12 recognizes another key figure in esoteric Gnostic tradition, James (see Perkins, 1980:141–156). He is the key to a Gnostic tradition of non-apostolic revelation.

4.62   Log. 114 returns to the issue of Petrine authority. The conclusion is commonly taken as a reference to union with the angelic aeon (Ménard: 210). However, the version of the tradition preserved in II Clement 12:5 suggests another reading. There the phrase "the male with the female; neither male nor female" applies to the relationship between men and women in the community: "When a brother sees a sister, he should have no thought of her as female; nor she of him as male." Log. 114 may represent a similar community rule about the status of men and women, a problem which must have been intensified by the encratitic environment of the Thomas tradition (cf. Koester, 1971a:126–143). The saying justifies the inclusion of women in the community—against orthodox slander that these so-called ascetics were really sexual libertines?

5.   None of the pronouncement stories in GTh are strong examples of the genre. One would hardly require such a genre to explain these sayings, if one did not have synoptic parallels to suggest that they were originally derived from pronouncement stories. Within their present context most of these passages are better described as "sayings interpretation," a form of dialogue exchange that played an important role in the development of Gnostic exegesis (Koester, 1979:551). This observation does not mean that some may not reflect non-canonical pronouncement stories that were circulating orally as sayings of Jesus, just as other logia have been derived from synoptic sayings traditions. However, the Gnostics show no appreciation of the dynamics of such stories even when they may still use them as controversy stories. Nor do they preserve primitive traditions. Rather, all seem to be understood as material for esoteric sayings interpretation and for the forms of Gnostic dialogue in which such interpretation was traced to the risen Jesus /6/.

NOTES

/1/   See Koester's plea for an investigation of Gnostic sayings material for evidence of earlier stages of the sayings tradition (Koester, 1978).

/2/   Lincoln's division of the sayings into instruction for the various levels of Gnostic initiate seems unnecessarily complex. However, it challenges interpreters to see the unity of the whole as an instruction dialogue for community use rather than as a haphazard collection of sayings.

/3/   Such problems plague all interpretations of GTh. See Schrage: 1–9, 19–27.

/4/   Ménard tries to make it a principle to interpret sayings so as to fit their introductions. This principle often requires rather more elaborate allegorization than we propose. Koester, on the other hand, suggests that a Johannine type of sayings tradition is reflected in Gnostic sayings exegesis.

/5/   We doubt (pace Lincoln) that this saying refers to baptism. "Stripping off the garment" can refer to spiritual resurrection and to the ascent of the soul after death. See Layton: 61f. for a discussion of the image and relevant epitaph material.

/6/   Part of this study was made possible by a Fellowship from the National Endowment for the Humanities, for which I am very grateful.

WORKS CONSULTED

Texts

Guillaumont, A., et al.
1959   *The Gospel according to Thomas.* New York: Harper & Row.

Robinson, James M.
1974   *Facsimile Edition of the Nag Hammadi Codices: Codex II.* Leiden: E. J. Brill.

Robinson, James M., et al.
1977   *The Nag Hammadi Library in English.* (NHLE) San Francisco: Harper & Row.

Studies

Beardslee, William
1972   "Proverbs in the Gospel of Thomas." Pp. 92–103 in *Studies in Early Christian Literature. Festschrift G. Widengren.* Ed. D. Aune. SNT 33. Leiden: E. J. Brill.

Fitzmyer, Joseph
1974(1959)   "The Oxyrhynchus *Logoi* of Jesus and the Coptic Gospel according to Thomas." Pp. 355–433 in *Essays on the Semitic Background of the New Testament.* Missoula, MT: Scholars.

Koester, Helmut
    1971a   "GNOMAI DIAPHOROI." Pp. 114–157 in *Trajectories through Early Christianity*. Philadelphia: Fortress.
    1971b   "One Jesus and Four Primitive Gospels." Pp. 158–204 in *Trajectories through Early Christianity*. Philadelphia: Fortress.
    1978   "Gnostic Writings as Witness for the Development of the Sayings Tradition." Paper read at the International Conference on Gnosticism, Yale University, 1978.
    1979   "Dialog und Spruchüberlieferung in den gnostischen Texten von Nag Hammadi." *EvTh* 39:532–556.

Koester, Helmut & Pagels, Elaine
    1978   "Report on the Dialogue of the Savior." Pp. 64–74 in *Nag Hammadi and Gnosis*. Ed. R. Wilson. NHS 14. Leiden: E. J. Brill.

Layton, Bentley
    1979   *The Gnostic Treatise on Resurrection from Nag Hammadi*. Missoula, MT: Scholars.

Lincoln, B.
    1977   "Thomas Gospel and Thomas Community: A New Approach to a Familiar Text." *NovT* 19:65–76.

Ménard, Jacques-É.
    1975   *L'Évangile selon Thomas*. NHS 5. Leiden: E. J. Brill.

Pagels, Elaine
    1973   *The Johannine Gospel in Gnostic Exegesis*. SBLMS 17. Nashville: Abingdon.
    1979   *The Gnostic Gospels*. New York: Random House.

Perkins, Pheme
    1974   "Peter in Gnostic Revelation." Pp. 1–13 in *Society of Biblical Literature Seminar Papers*, vol. 2. Missoula, MT: Scholars.
    1980   *The Gnostic Dialogue*. New York: Paulist.

Rudolph, Kurt
    1968   "Der gnostische Dialog als literarische Genus." *Probleme der koptischen Literatur*. Wiss. Beitr. Martin-Luther Univ. Halle-Wittenberg. 1968/1 [K2]:85–107.

Schrage, W.
    1964   *Das Verhältnis des Thomas-Evangeliums zur synoptischen Tradition*. BZNW 29. Berlin: Alfred Töpelmann.

Wilder, Amos
    1971   *Early Christian Rhetoric*. Cambridge, MA: Harvard University.

EXAMPLES OF PRONOUNCEMENT STORIES IN EARLY CHRISTIAN APOCRYPHAL LITERATURE

William D. Stroker
Drew University

ABSTRACT

Relatively few examples of pronouncement stories are found in early Christian apocryphal literature. The materials surveyed for this study are those treated or referred to in standard works on "New Testament apocrypha," with the exception of the Nag Hammadi Codices, Codices Brucianus and Askewianus, and Papyrus Berolinensis 8502. Conclusions regarding the type and frequency of use of pronouncement stories in this literature are difficult, particularly in light of the fragmentary nature of much of the material. The examples found come primarily from the "gospel" genre. The apocryphal acts contain very few narratives in pronouncement story form. The examples found fall primarily into the categories of objection, correction, and inquiry of Professor Tannehill's typology. No examples of quests or descriptions were found.

0.   Early Christian apocryphal literature is a cover category for a large group of diverse writings. This is not the place to engage in a discussion of the scope and appropriateness of the designation. For the Work Group on the Pronouncement Story it has functioned primarily to indicate a division of labor. The documents studied in search of pronouncement stories are those treated or referred to in such standard works as Hennecke-Schneemelcher's *New Testament Apocrypha* and James' *The Apocryphal New Testament*, with the exception of those materials contained in the Nag Hammadi Codices, Codices Brucianus and Askewianus, and Papyrus Berolinensis 8502.

The following treatment employs the typology developed in the Work Group under the leadership of Professor Tannehill. I will give a brief indication of the identifying characteristics of the categories within the typology of which examples have been found. For a more complete description, see Tannehill's discussion elsewhere in this volume. Unless otherwise indicated, translations of the Greek and Latin texts are my own.

1.   Objections. The basic characteristics of this category are: (a) an objection to a statement or act of the central figure, and (b) a response which justifies the central figure's position and which may also criticize, correct, or even rebuke the stance of the objector. Three examples of this category have been found, and a possible fourth.

1.1   Now one day as John was sitting (there) a partridge flew by and came and played in the dust before him; and John was amazed as he saw it. But a certain priest, who was one of his hearers, came and went in to John and saw the partridge playing in the dust before him. And he was offended and said to him, "Can such a man, at his age, take pleasure in a partridge playing in the dust?" But John knew in the spirit what he was thinking, and said to him, "It would be better for you, my son, to watch a partridge playing in the dust and not to foul yourself with shameful and impious practices. For he who waits for the conversion and repentance of all men has brought you here for this purpose. For I have no need of a partridge playing in the dust; for the partridge is your own soul."

When the elder heard this and saw that he was not unknown but that the Apostle of Christ had told him all that was in his heart, he fell on his face to the ground and cried out, saying, "Now I know that God dwells in you, blessed John! How happy is the man who has not tempted God in you; for the man who tempts you tempts the untemptable. And he begged him to pray for him; and (John) instructed him and gave him injunctions (or, "canons") and sent him away to his house, and glorified God who is (Lord) over all.

Acts of John 56–57 (trans. from Hennecke-Schneemelcher 2:242–243; Greek text in Lipsius-Bonnet 2.1:178–179)

1.2   It is told that the most blessed Evangelist John, when he was quietly stroking a partridge with his hands, suddenly saw one in the habit of a hunter coming to him. He wondered that a man of such repute and fame should demean himself to such small and humble amusements, and said: Art thou that John whose eminent and widespread fame hath enticed me also with great desire to know thee? Why then art thou taken up with such mean amusements? The blessed John said to him: What is that which thou carriest in thy hand? A bow, said he. And why, said he, dost thou not bear it about always stretched? He answered him: I must not, lest by constant bending the strength of its vigour be wrung and grow soft and perish, and when there is need that the arrows be shot with much strength at some beast, the strength being lost by excess of continual tension, a forceful blow cannot be dealt. Just so, said the blessed John, let not this little and brief relaxation of my mind offend thee, young man, for unless it doth sometimes ease and relax by some remission the force of its tension, it will grow slack through unbroken rigour and will not be able to obey the power of the spirit.

John Cassian, Conlationes 24.21 (trans. from James: 241; Latin text in Petschenig: 697–698).

1.21   Despite the obvious differences, the progression of the narratives in John Cassian and Acts of John 56 (Acts of John 56 and 57 taken together will be treated later) is basically the same. We probably have independent developments of a common tradition. In both passages someone objects, verbally or 'to himself,' to John's amusement with the partridge. The response by John contains not only a defense but also an indication of a deeper significance. The response in the first narrative is *ad hominem*; the partridge in the dirt symbolizes the condition of the soul of the one who raised the objection. The second makes a general point about the necessity of mental relaxation. The second narrative has a more complex development, with its dialogue between John and the hunter, which functions to prepare for and also illustrate the point made in John's concluding words.

1.22   The Acts of John 56, taken alone, is a clear example of an objection story. The parallel in John Cassian indicates it could have had an independent status at an earlier stage in the tradition. The narrative continues in section 57, however, and the two sections together may be viewed as a more complex pronouncement story. Section 56 with John's successful response to the objection now functions as a setting for a commendation of John by the elder-priest. Commendations in which the central figure receives rather than gives commendation may be viewed, following the suggestion of Vernon Robbins, as a subcategory termed "laudations." Section 57 also contains a final sentence which, with its mention of John's instructing and sending the man home and praising God, rounds off the entire episode. Sentences like this are not integral to pronouncement stories as such but can function to help incorporate them into larger literary contexts.

1.3   It says: The other rich man said to him: "Master, what good thing must I do that I may live?" He said to him: "Man, do what is in the law and the prophets." He answered him: "I have done that." He said to him: "Go and sell all you possess and distribute it among the poor, and come, follow me." But the rich man then began to scratch his head, and it did not please him. And the Lord said to him: "How can you say, 'I have done what is in the law and the prophets?' For it is written in the law: 'Love your neighbor as yourself;' and behold, many of your brothers, sons of Abraham, are clothed in filth and die of hunger, while your house is full of many good things, and nothing at all comes out of it for them." And he turned and said to Simon, his disciple, who was sitting by him: "Simon, son of Jonah, it is easier for a camel to go through the eye of a needle than for a rich man to enter into the kingdom of heaven."

Gospel of the Nazaraeans, from Origen, *On Matt.* 15.14
(Klostermann: 389–390)

1.31   The version of this in Mark 10:17–22 parr. is a clear example of Tannehill's quest category. The major difference between the quoted version and those in the synoptics is Jesus' trenchant rebuke which challenges the veracity of the man's claim that he has done what is required by the law and the prophets. The initial positive portrayal of the man is thus virtually cancelled (though the characterization was less positive to begin with than those of the synoptics, particularly Mark's). The only vestige is the legitimacy of the question which he posed. The narrative may, therefore, not have enough of the distinguishing characteristics to qualify as a quest.

1.32   Another view of the passage would treat it as an objection. The setting, then, would include the initial dialogue and culminate in the indication that the man began to scratch his head and was displeased, that is, objected to Jesus' command that he "go and sell all. . . ." Jesus' rebuke of the man and the metaphorical saying addressed to Simon constitute his response to the objection. This approach would appear to do more justice to the special characteristics of the passage than would an attempt to treat it as a modified or hybrid quest.

1.4   A "Borderline" Objection.

> And he took them and brought them into the place of purification itself and walked about in the temple. And a certain Pharisee, a chief priest named Levi, approached and spoke with them and said to the Savior: "Who permitted you to walk in this place of purification and to view these holy vessels, without having washed and without your disciples' having washed even their feet? On the contrary, while still defiled, you have walked in this temple which is a clean place, in which no one who has not washed himself and changed his clothes walks or dares view these holy vessels." Immediately the Savior stood still, along with the disciples, and answered him: "Are you who are here in the temple therefore clean?" He said: "I am clean, for I have washed in David's pool and have gone down by one stair and come up by the other and have put on clean, white clothes, and then I came and looked at these holy vessels." The Savior answered and said to him: "Woe to you blind who do not see. You have washed yourself in these poured-out waters in which dogs and swine have wallowed night and day, and you have washed and wiped the outer skin which harlots and flute girls also anoint, wash, wipe, and beautify for the lust of men, whereas within they are full of scorpions and wickedness of every kind. But I and my disciples, whom you say have not washed, have been washed in waters of eternal life which come down from [heaven]. But woe to those who . . ."
>
> Oxyrhynchus Papyrus 840 (Grenfell and Hunt: 6–7)

1.41   There is some question as to whether this narrative should be designated a pronouncement story. It is longer and the dialogue more wordy than usually is the case. The narrative does not move quickly and effectively toward a single pronouncement. The end of the episode is not preserved, so we cannot be confident the narrative reached its climax in Jesus' response to the objection. Nonetheless, the basic structure of situation-objection-response is clearly visible. We may have here an elaborated pronouncement story in which the usual economy of language is not operative, particularly in the dialogue. Or we may have, as part of a longer, more developed narrative, an episode which involves objection and response but whose development is distinct from that of the pronouncement story proper.

2.   Corrections. More examples of corrections have been found in the documents studied than of any other category. In examples of this category the climactic utterance corrects a position taken or implied in the setting.

The setting may consist of a statement, request, or question addressed to the central figure, or it may be a description of an action or situation.

2.1 But, he said, when the apostles asked how the Jewish prophets were to be regarded who were thought to have proclaimed in the past his coming, our Lord, disturbed that they still held this conception, answered: "You have forsaken the living one who is before you and speak about the dead."

Augustine, *Contra adv. legis et proph.* 2.4.14 (Migne, *PL*, 42:647)

2.11 This is a clear example of the correction category, as is shown in the narrative by the indication of what the assessment of the prophets was, the notice that Jesus was disturbed to learn the apostles still had this view, as well as by the corrective response itself. The close parallel to this passage in Thomas 52 is also a correction.

2.2 On the same day he saw a man working on the Sabbath and said to him: "Man, if you know what you are doing, you are blessed. But if you do not know, you are cursed and a transgressor of the law."

Codex D after Luke 6:4

2.21 The description of the scene to which Jesus responds has no interest in things such as the motivation of the man or the type of work. The response also gives little insight into these matters but challenges the person to consider the situation with great care. The response points to two possibilities, which is unusual in pronouncement stories. Two judgments are given, one of commendation, the other of correction. It is tempting to view the narrative as a hybrid of these two categories, but it is more likely a correction story. The two judgments taken together correct an implied assumption that working on the Sabbath is simply permitted. Also, the rhetorical weight of the passage as a whole seems to fall on the second, the corrective, response.

2.3 Behold, the mother of the Lord and his brothers said to him: "John the Baptist baptizes for the remission of sins; let us go and be baptised by him." But he said to them: "Wherein have I sinned, that I should go and be baptized by him? Unless this very thing which I have said is ignorance."

Gospel of the Nazaraeans, from Jerome, *Dial. adv. Pelag.* 3.2 (Migne, *PL*, 23:570–571)

2.31 The quotation by Jerome is in the form of a pronouncement story. Within the Gospel of the Nazaraeans, however, it was part of a more extended narrative which probably included an account of the baptism itself. Until the last sentence the narrative proceeds as a clear correction. The position of Jesus' mother and brothers implies he is in need of the remission of sins. Jesus' initial question corrects this by challenging the assumption (Thomas 104 provides a partial parallel; Jesus responds to the suggestion that he fast and pray with analogous words). The second sentence of the response in Jerome's quotation, the exact meaning of which is uncertain, complicates matters somewhat. It may seem to blunt the force of the correction. Nonetheless, the passage is best viewed as a correction story, challenging a misunderstanding of why Jesus was baptized.

2.4   Peter, speaking to a (man) who bitterly complained at the death of his daughter, said "So many assaults of the devil, so many struggles with the body, so many disasters of the world she has escaped; and you shed tears, as if you did not know what you yourself have undergone (i.e. what you have gained)."

> Codex Cambrai 254 (trans. from Hennecke-Schnee-melcher 2:279; Latin text in de Bruyne, 1908:153)

2.41   This brief narrative shows no interest in the daughter or in the circumstances of her death. Attention is focused on the reaction of the father and the implied assumption behind his position. The words of Peter give an alternate perspective which corrects the assumption and also mildy rebukes the father.

2.42   A partial parallel to this narrative is found in Ps. Titus' *De disp. sanct.*

Consider and take note of the happening about which the following account informs us: A peasant had a girl who was a virgin. She was also his only daughter, and therefore he besought Peter to offer a prayer for her. After he had prayed, the apostle said to the father that the Lord would bestow upon her what was expedient for her soul. Immediately, the girl fell down dead. O reward worthy and ever pleasing to God, to escape the shamelessness of the flesh and to break the pride of the blood! But this distrustful old man, failing to recognize the worth of the heavenly grace, i.e. the divine blessing, besought Peter again that his only daughter be raised from the dead. And some days later, after she had been raised, a man who passed himself off as a believer came into the house of the old man to stay with him, and seduced the girl, and the two of them never appeared again.

> Ps. Titus, *De disp. sanct.* (Trans. from Hennecke-Schnee-melcher 2:146-147; Latin text in de Bruyne, 1925:50)

2.43   The affinities between the first half of this story and the one quoted in 2.4 are enough to suggest that they are independent developments of a common tradition. One may well question, however, whether the version in Ps. Titus is in the form of a pronouncement story. The event which drives the point home and which forms the climax of the narrative is not accomplished by Peter, nor is it a result of Peter's prayer. When an act is the climactic element of a pronouncement story, it must be more closely related to the central figure than is the case here. The passage may perhaps be viewed as an expansion of a pronouncement story, which is still visible in the first half. The coupling of Peter's assurance that the Lord would do what was best for the daughter's soul with her immediate death corrects the expectations and assumptions of the father.

If, however, the entire passage in Ps. Titus were to be considered a pronouncement story, it would be an example of an objection. The father objects not only to his daughter's death, but also to the understanding that this was "expedient for her soul," and requests that his daughter be raised. The raising of the daughter and the subsequent events are the "response" to the objection, though obviously not a verbal response. The better assessment of the passage is to view it as containing a pronouncement story in the beginning. The elaboration of the narrative gives negative reinforcement to the message. The mode of elaboration, however, leaves the resulting narrative not in the form of a pronouncement story.

2.5 When Salome asked, "How long will death have power?" the Lord said, "As long as you women bear children"—not as if life were bad and creation evil, but as teaching the sequence of nature. For death always follows birth.

> Gospel of the Egyptians, from Clement Alex., *Strom.* 3.6.45 (Stählin-Früchtel: 217)

2.51   Clement's interpretative comments point this passage toward the category of inquiry. The question would appear to be open, its validity accepted, and an answer given. Clement's interpretation, however, blunts the pointed nature of the response, which appears to correct an implied assumption behind the question and which also may contain elements of rebuke.

3.   A Possible Commendation. Commendations are the counterpart to corrections. The response often goes beyond simple approval to state a general principle or to point out a significance not immediately apparent in the setting itself.

3.1 For when she said, "I have done well then in not having borne children," as if it were improper to engage in procreation, then the Lord answered and said, "Eat every plant, but do not eat the one which contains bitterness."

> Gospel of the Egyptians, from Clement Alex., *Strom.* 3.9.66 (Stählin-Früchtel: 226)

3.11   Clement interprets this passage as a correction, as is seen in his inserted comment and in the broader context in which he uses the quotation. The encratite tendencies of the Gospel of the Egyptians, however, are well known. If Clement's comment and overall interpretation are removed, then the metaphorical saying could be considered a commendation of the perspective expressed by Salome.

4.   Inquiries. In this category an open question or request is put to the central figure. The appropriateness of this is accepted, and a response is given. The following two versions of essentially the same tradition are clear examples.

4.1   When Salome asked when the things would be known that she had inquired
about, the Lord said, "When you (pl.) have trampled on the garment of shame
and when the two become one and the male with the female is neither male nor
female."

> Gospel of the Egyptians, from Clement Alex., *Strom.*
> 3.13.92 (Stählin-Früchtel: 238)

4.2   For when the Lord himself was asked by someone when his kingdom would
come, he said, "When the two shall be one and the outside as the inside and the
male with the female neither male nor female."

> 2 Clement 12.2 (Funk-Bihlmeyer: 76)

5.   Results. Relatively few examples of pronouncement stories were
found in the documents studied. Further, no examples of quests or
descriptions were found. These factors do not lead to the conclusion that
pronouncement stories were infrequent in early Christian apocryphal
literature. The Nag Hammadi documents were not included in this survey.
The Gospel of Thomas contains pronouncement stories, if the responses by
Jesus to the questions and statements of the disciples and others are
considered to belong to this genre. Sections 34, 54, and 55 of the Gospel of
Philip are also pronouncement stories. Further, our knowledge of much of
the apocryphal literature is quite fragmentary. The Jewish-Christian gospels
and the Gospel of the Egyptians contained pronouncement stories, as is
evident from the few quotations preserved, and it is not unreasonable to
assume that there were more. The documents of which P. Eg. 2 and P. Oxy.
840 and 1224 are parts also likely contained more pronouncement stories.
The "gospel" category of apocryphal literature thus gives evidence which
would point to an extensive use of the pronouncement story, though not all
types of gospels would be expected to have made comparable use.
     Within other categories of apocryphal literature, the situation seems to
be otherwise. We would perhaps not expect the pronouncement story to be
frequently employed in apocryphal epistles and apocalypses. The
pronouncement story *could* have been used, however, in the apocryphal acts
of the apostles. These acts often contain series of episodes relating actions
and teachings of the central figures, but the combination of narrative and
dialogue is quite different from that of the pronouncement story. The
passages concerning Peter and John quoted above are only partly exceptions.
There is evidence of independent circulation of both traditions, and their
locations within the "finished" acts are tenuous at best. It is possible that the
authors of the acts had at their disposal briefer, isolated units of tradition,
some of which may have been in pronouncement story form. Nonetheless, it
is quite apparent that these authors tend not to preserve and employ
traditions about the apostles in this form. The same holds for the pseudo-
Clementine literature.

WORKS CONSULTED

Bruyne, Donatien de
1908   "Nouveaux fragments des Actes de Pierre, de Paul, de Jean, d'André, et de l'Apocalypse d'Élie." *Revue Bénédictine* 25:149–160.
1925   "Epistula Titi, discipuli Pauli, de dispositione sanctimonii." *Revue Bénédictine* 37:47–72.

Funk, Franz X. von, and Bihlmeyer, Karl
1956   *Die apostolischen Väter.* Tübingen: J. C. B. Mohr (Paul Siebeck).

Grenfell, Bernard P., and Hunt, Arthur S.
1908   *The Oxyrhynchus Papyri,* vol. 5. London: Egypt Exploration Fund.

Hennecke, Edgar, and Schneemelcher, Wilhelm
1963, 1965   *New Testament Apocrypha,* vols. 1 and 2. Philadelphia: Westminster.

James, Montague R.
1924   *The Apocryphal New Testament.* Oxford: Clarendon.

Klostermann, Erich
1935   *Origenes Werke,* Bd. 10, *Origenes Matthäuserklärung.* GCS 40. Leipzig: J. C. Hinrichs.

Lipsius, Richard A., and Bonnet, Max
1959   *Acta Apostolorum Apocrypha,* Bd. 2, 1. Hildesheim: Georg Olms.

Migne, Jacques P.
1844ff.   *Patrologiae cursus completus, Series Latina,* vols. 23, 42. Paris.

Petschenig, Michael
1966   *Iohannis Cassiani Conlationes XXIII.* CSEL 13. New York: Johnson Reprint Corp.

Stählin, Otto, and Früchtel, Ludwig
1960   *Clemens Alexandrinus,* Bd. 2. 3rd ed. GCS 52(15). Berlin: Akademie.